Praise for *B_____*

"The harrowing real-life stories of three girls who turned their experiences as sex-trafficked children into a fight to destroy the practice…The girls' stories could be too devastating to read save for each tale's conclusion, detailing the efforts these women have made to rescue girls and eliminate childhood slavery… Harrowing, yes—and inspiring."
—*Kirkus Reviews*

"If we want real, systemic change, we must listen to survivors. Abby Sher shares these survivors' truths with care and compassion, highlighting the courage and resilience of each woman. This is an excellent read for anyone who believes that ending exploitation is possible."
—Lauren Hersh, *Equality Now*

"This book is invaluable for young people to learn about not just the horrors of sex trafficking but also how victims can become survivors and finally leaders."
—Prof. Ruchira Gupta, *Founder and President of Apne Aap Women Worldwide*

"*Breaking Free* is a courageous and compassionate exploration of a deeply difficult subject matter, filled with hope and solutions as well as important truths. I would say it should be required reading for every high school, but really, it should be required reading for every HUMAN."
—Alysia Reiner, *Actress (Orange Is the New Black)*

"These searing, harrowing stories tell us the dark truth of the lives of enslaved girls and women, our own sisters and daughters. In Abby Sher's generous, thoughtful prose, they also become tales of unbelievable courage, hope, and triumph."
—Jennifer Finney Boylan, *author of She's Not There*

"They speak for the voiceless, the scared, and the still enslaved. They speak for people everywhere with a dream to better the world… This is a must read for everyone."
—Missy Taylor, *reviewer at A Midsummer Night's Read*

BREAKING FREE

FREE

TRUE STORIES OF GIRLS WHO ESCAPED MODERN SLAVERY

Abby Sher

BARRON'S

ISBN: 978-1-4380-0453-2

All inquiries should be addressed to:
Barron's Educational Series, Inc.
250 Wireless Boulevard
Hauppauge, NY 11788
www.barronseduc.com

Some names have been changed in this book to
protect the privacy of the individuals involved.

Library of Congress Control Number: 2014902515

Printed in the United States of America
9 8 7 6 5 4 3 2 1

Contents

for Samantha,
who taught me how we are all connected

Preface

Don't call me hero. Call me human.

When I started this book, I thought sex trafficking happened only far away—in small villages with no running water and maybe the occasional light bulb for electricity. I know that sounds ignorant and kind of snooty. Let me explain: I grew up in a sleepy town in Westchester County, New York, where my greatest fear was someone else wearing the same dress as me to the junior prom. I knew all my neighbors, my mom was in the PTA, and I was taught that I'd be safe as long as I didn't take candy from strangers.

I was so wrong.

Sex trafficking happens all over the world, including here. Sex trafficking is defined as the act of forcing, coercing, or conning someone into performing any sexual act. According to U.S. law, anyone younger than eighteen who is selling or being sold for sex acts is a victim of sex trafficking, whether it's done by force or not.

The girls and women in these pages are not only brave survivors of sex trafficking; they are also inspiring leaders in the anti-trafficking movement. After they broke free, they chose to dedicate their lives to activism to help other sex-trafficking victims become empowered survivors, too. They each work every day with the hope of creating a world where sex trafficking has been stopped once and for all. They speak to everyone from convicted traffickers to the leaders of the United Nations, because they know that change can only happen when we all work together.

The first story comes from Somaly Mam, who grew up in the deep forests of Cambodia. After being abandoned by her parents, she was sold into sexual slavery by someone who claimed to be her grandfather. Today, she runs The Somaly Mam Foundation, one of the most successful organizations in the anti-trafficking movement—freeing and educating girls and women just like her.

The second account is from Minh Dang, a young woman who grew up in a quiet suburb of California. Behind closed doors, her parents were abusing her and selling her to local brothels for most of her life. Minh is now very well known for her work as an anti-trafficking advocate and recently got an award at the White House for being a Champion of Change.

The third tale is from Maria Suarez, a Mexican immigrant who was not only held captive by her trafficker in the United States for several years, but was then imprisoned for a crime she didn't commit. The first thing Maria did after getting out of prison was to start counseling victims of abuse and trafficking. She is now starting the Maria Suarez Foundation, which will prevent abuse and rescue and rehabilitate survivors.

For every person in these pages, there are thousands more. I met a lot of survivors, activists, lawyers, and counselors who talked to me but didn't want to be quoted in this book because it could jeopardize someone's safety. A lot of girls and women who are just breaking free of the sex-trafficking nightmare cannot risk being named. But even when I didn't quote them in these pages, I did hear their stories gratefully, and I hope I do justice to their words about what it was like to get out, how they want the world to see them, and where they need to go from here.

Everyone who agreed to be named in this book did so willingly. Sometimes I used pseudonyms when people requested them. When I couldn't be in the same room as someone to hear her story—like with Somaly Mam—we shared ideas over e-mail. I wrote Somaly's story as if I were inside her head, so I could be as close as possible to her experience. But of course, we can never know exactly what anyone is thinking, so it's important to note that while every facet of the story is true, it is my interpretation of Somaly's journey.

With Minh and Maria, I had the great privilege of sitting next to them in cafés as they relayed their stories. It was hard for me to believe that these events really happened to them and that they were here to tell me their tales. How could these women who look calm, cool, and even hopeful be sitting here with me, sipping milkshakes while reliving their harrowing pasts?

It's much easier to see survivors of sex trafficking as superhuman warriors, or their stories as too horrible to be true, but that only makes it easier to think of sex trafficking as someone else's problem. Superheroes wear jetpacks and capes and appear in comic books. They don't need help, except for maybe a sidekick to dust them off when they fall.

Talking to these women made it clear that I had to rethink my image of them and of myself. As I often heard them say, most importantly: *We are human, just like you.* No matter where we come from, no matter what brought us to today, we are not so different at all.

We all get skinned knees and cry. We all have at least one knock-knock joke that makes us laugh. We all hurt and heal and live in frightening uncertainty, though it looks different to everybody. And we can make this world a lot brighter if we're honest and loving. To make a real difference, we have to listen and start seeing how we are one and the same.

Somaly and I have both found the most intense calm in the rush of a waterfall. We both feel loved when someone sings us a lullaby. While I never had to fend for myself in the woods like her, I do know what it's like to lose a parent and ache from loneliness.

Minh and I both collect stationery and stickers. Just because Minh's parents started selling her for sex on a street corner when she was ten years old, while mine fed me chicken soup in a white house with tulips in our garden, doesn't mean that we are members of different species.

Maria and I have the same favorite dessert: peanut butter milkshakes. Maria earned her GED in prison at the same time I got to perform in the spring play in high school. That doesn't make either of our educations fuller or more meaningful.

These women didn't break free from sex trafficking because of any superpowers. They didn't get to fly away in a rocket ship or on some magic carpet. They made it out because they are and always will be *human*. We all deserve to be treated as humans, not as property. And when nobody was treating them *humanely*, they found a single friend, a mentor, or an inner voice that screamed *I believe in you!*

Though the first story comes from a small village with no running water or light bulbs, I hope you'll still see how Somaly's hopes, dreams, and fears could be any little girl's—anywhere in the world. I hope you'll see how the cycle of human trafficking affects us all, and that to stop it we must believe in one another and in ourselves.

I hope you'll read these words and believe that we all can and *will* break free.

This is how it starts, by reading one story and seeing how it's your story, too.

And yours.

And yours.

And mine.

And ours.

Somaly Mam

> **"** ████████████████████
>
> *Of course you can't forget it, but I am sure that you can forgive and turn a page of your life with new light and hope.*
>
> ████████████████████ **"**

~ Somaly Mam

A Forest Called Home

For Somaly Mam, the most wonderful time was when the rice harvest was done. Many villages in the forests of Cambodia came together then. There was wild dancing and singing around a bonfire so tall it licked the sky. The elders sacrificed a buffalo to the native spirits, and everyone passed around big jugs of rice wine, sipping it through bamboo straws. Somaly loved these harvest celebrations so much. Here she was part of a family. It didn't matter if it was not her real mother or father or sister or brother. She was a little girl surrounded by people who loved her.

While the singing was winding down, Somaly strung a hammock between two trees. She lay down and watched the bonfire smoke swirl around the moon. She felt like she was floating on everyone's song. Festival nights were her favorite because she could hear the stars laughing. She knew she was safe in this forest she called home.

Somaly was born in a rural village called Bou Sra around 1970. She never knew the exact month or year. She didn't even know what her name was then. Her parents left her as a baby when a civil war was breaking out, but the war never came to Bou Sra. It was a quiet pocket of land among the towering trees and the roaring waterfalls of northeastern Cambodia.

In the center of the village was a circle of bamboo huts. Everyone inside those huts looked after one another. Even though Somaly had no roof to call her own, and no one to call her daughter, she knew she would always have food to eat and a floor to sleep on during the rainy season. She didn't try to figure out *why* her parents abandoned her, or *how* she could have lived a different life if they'd stayed. She couldn't live in *what if*s or else she would get too sad.

All the children in Bou Sra got to run through the forest naked or in clothes they made out of leaves and vines. Somaly was a great forager. She knew which mushrooms were safe to eat, which insects were the meatiest, and how to follow a bee to its honey source without getting stung. Whenever she caught a wood-land animal, she brought it to a kind man named Taman so he could cook it for her.

Taman and his wife and children always made room for Somaly in their one-room hut. They called her Non, or "Little One." Somaly treasured those nights in their cheery home. She loved it when Taman's wife bathed her. After the bath, Taman's wife rubbed pig's fat into Somaly's hair so it felt smooth and warm. She also sang beautiful songs that Somaly tucked deep inside her skin. Those nights were Somaly's only memories of being loved and held by a mom. Even if it wasn't her own.

Somaly lived in Bou Sra for around nine years. In the rest of Cambodia, the civil war kept gaining steam. Most Cambodians called this time The Troubles. The Khmer Rouge political party and a brutal dictator named Pol Pot took over with their loyal soldiers. About one in five people were executed or starved to death. Practically everyone was forced into some sort of labor camp. Pol Pot closed schools and hospitals. He forbade anyone to read, drive cars, or even wear glasses—anything that he thought of as too modern or threatening to his complete control. Bou Sra wasn't modern at all. The people of Bou Sra had no money, no medicine, nothing connecting them to the Western world. So Pol Pot left them unharmed.

Somaly wasn't fighting in any war, but she did have a vicious enemy called loneliness. Besides the harvest festivals and nights with Taman's family, it was hard always fending for herself. When the other children were called home in the evening, Somaly had to invent her own playmates and games. She played hide and seek with small animals. She climbed to the highest limbs of each tree in one swoop. Sometimes she just stood still under the waterfalls for hours as the water pounded into the rocks and the sky tumbled by in a rush of speckled sunlight.

At night, in her hammock under the inky sky, Somaly asked the birds to tell her bedtime stories. She told her deepest secrets and hopes to the treetops. She liked to imagine their branches were her mother's arms. Their leaves fluttering in lullabies sang just for her.

> **"** I always feel hope even in the darkness, because I think when you are still alive, even for [a] few more minutes, you have a chance to have hope. Without hope, how can you survive? **"**
>
> ~ Somaly Mam

Blue Rubber Flip-Flops

When Somaly was about nine years old, Taman introduced her to an older man who said to call him Grandfather. This was a way of showing him respect as an elder, and Somaly believed he could in fact be her grandfather. Grandfather also said he would return Somaly to her parents if she followed him out of the forest. He seemed kind, and Taman said it was a good idea because nobody in Bou Sra could really look after her. So, Somaly left with him.

Grandfather was completely silent as they walked together for days. She didn't know if she should try to talk to him or ask him how he knew her parents. She wanted to be respectful, but she was also very eager to know where they were going and to get there already.

Pretty soon, Grandfather made it clear even without words that this trip was not what she'd expected. They came to a crowd that was gathering around a logging truck. Somaly had never seen a truck before and she backed away. Grandfather scowled at her and swung a fist into her face. Then he hauled her onto the truck as if she were nothing more than a stack of logs, too.

As she rubbed her sore cheek, she began to realize what was really going on. This man was no grandfatherly figure, and he was not here to help her. She was days and miles away from anyone or anything familiar, and getting farther by the minute.

When they got off the truck, they arrived at a crumbling bamboo hut in a village called Thlok Chhrov. Grandfather told her she was his servant now. She had to cook, clean, wash his clothes, and fetch his water from the Mekong River in heavy metal buckets. The buckets cut into the backs of her legs, making them hot and swollen. Grandfather also made Somaly cook and clean for his neighbors, so he would have money for drinking and gambling.

Sometimes at night, Somaly woke up to find Grandfather's hands climbing up her chest. Whenever this happened, she bolted out the door. She ran to the riverbank to hide in a docked fishing boat or under a pile of dry rice stalks. She didn't dare tell anyone what was going on. Most of the people in Thlok Chhrov shouted insults at Somaly because her skin was darker than theirs and because she was too thin from not having enough to eat. She waited until the deep of night to talk to her new best friend, the river.

Somaly asked the river to guide her and protect her. The water babbled back but it gave her no answers. She knew she could not give up hope, but who would come to rescue this raggedy orphan with dark skin and no name besides Little One?

She found her first flicker of hope in a pair of blue rubber flip-flops with thorns and rocks poking through the heels.

One of the old women who hired Somaly to fetch her water from the river every morning saw Somaly's sore feet and put the blue flip-flops by her door. When Somaly showed up one morning, the woman didn't say a word. She just pointed to the shoes and smiled. There were two big holes in the heels and the flip-flops barely stayed on Somaly's feet, but she loved them.

Pock, pock, pock.

Somaly marched along the woman's mud floor and laughed at the silly sound of the bottoms slapping against it. Somaly didn't know how to thank her.

Servants were supposed to stay silent always. She hoped her smile was enough.

Pock, pock, pock, pock.

It was the most noise she made from the day Grandfather brought her to this miserable village. Visiting the old woman and wearing those flip-flops even for an hour each morning became the highlight of Somaly's day.

FICTION: ▰▰▰▰▰▰▰▰▰▰▰▰▰▰▰▰▰

An "orange woman" is a young girl who sells oranges in the public gardens of Cambodia.

FACT: ▰▰▰▰▰▰▰▰▰▰▰▰▰▰▰▰▰

Whenever a man buys an orange, he also buys the right to fondle the girl. Add another twenty-five cents and he can have sex with her, too.

The Sagging Birdhouse

Somaly was very careful not to get in anybody's way in Thlok Chhrov. She did her work diligently and talked only to the Mekong River about how homesick and lost she felt. But there was a boy who worked in the fields nearby, and he often hid in the rice stalks, too. One day he told Somaly in whispers that he knew a place where they could get rice and broth and the people were so kind. Somaly had to swear to keep it a secret before he would let her come.

He took her to a hut that was built on stilts. It leaned over like a giant sagging birdhouse. Inside was a schoolteacher named Mam Khon and his wife, Pen Navy. The floor of their home was covered with children chatting, giggling, and slurping soup. Mam Khon and Pen Navy welcomed Somaly. They didn't ask her any questions. They didn't make her fetch their water or wash their clothes. Pen Navy dished out a bowl of rice for Somaly. She ate it so quickly and gratefully, she felt her whole body hiccup.

Soon Somaly went to Mam Khon's hut every day. Grandfather never knew because Somaly was always careful to get her work done first before slipping through the rice stalks to the sagging birdhouse. Pen Navy was a baker and let Somaly help her with the cakes she sold. Sometimes she even let Somaly eat one on the way to market.

Somaly didn't know how to thank this beautiful, generous family. Mam Khon said she could call him Father and Pen Navy, Mother. They had six children of their own. Somaly shyly began to call them sisters. The family clothed her, fed her, and took care of her when she was sick. She dreamed of hiding under the stilts of their house so Grandfather could never find her again. But he expected her home every morning and evening to cook his meals and bring her earnings to him. She could not bear the thought of getting her new family in trouble.

One day, Pen Navy asked Somaly if she wanted to go to the school where Mam Khon taught. It wasn't much more than a floor with a thatched roof to keep out the rain; there weren't even any walls on the sides. Somaly knew it was near their home because she heard children singing and laughing there all the time. She wanted to go very badly. She wanted to dress in the blue skirt and white shirt that all the other girls wore. Somaly told Pen Navy she didn't know how it could ever work, but that she would love to go.

That was all Pen Navy needed to hear. Somaly never found out how he did it, but Mam Khon persuaded Grandfather to let her go to school. The rules were that she had to get up and finish her work before seven each morning. She went to school from seven until eleven. Then she had to go back and either work in the fields or do military training. She washed her uniform in the river, prepared Grandfather's supper, and did his cleaning and chores. Then she willed her eyes to stay open as she studied her schoolbooks under the last shred of moonlight. (Grandfather rarely had enough money for an oil lamp.)

School was the greatest gift for Somaly. For those four hours of school each day she was free. Free to speak out loud and learn new words. Free to read books and write numbers in a line. Free to open her mouth and her eyes and her mind in a thousand new directions.

Best of all, on the first day of school, Mam Khon told the other teacher, Mr. Chai: "She's my daughter. I lost her in The Troubles, but now I've found her. She's mine."

Somaly was shocked when she heard him. She didn't think it was true, but she ached for it to be so. Mam Khon also told Mr. Chai that her name was Mam Somaly. Mam, because she was part of Mam Khon's family. Somaly meant "The Necklace of Flowers Lost in the Virgin Forest."

Somaly was so ecstatic about her new name she wanted to shout it to the skies. She was eleven years old, and for the first time, she knew who she was.

Nobody is ready for everything. I always encourage the girls to prepare not only for good things, but also to be ready for failure, and ready to stand up and try again.

"

~Somaly Mam

Lamp Oil and Candy

Grandfather finally saved up enough to buy lamp oil. Or at least that's what he told her. He sent Somaly to pick up the oil at the Chinese merchant's shop. When she got there, the merchant seemed confused at first. She didn't have any money with her, or even a bag of rice to trade for the oil. But then the merchant nodded his head with a slow, strange smile.

Somaly didn't know what it was about that smile, but it made her shiver.

Somaly knew this merchant pretty well. He and his wife were usually kind and gave her a small cake or a piece of candy when she came to buy oil for Grandfather. Only this time, the merchant's wife was nowhere in sight.

The merchant gave Somaly a cake and told her to follow him into the storeroom. He quickly pushed her onto a pile of rice sacks, then held her down and beat her until she was bleary. Somaly lay there, frozen in shock. Then the merchant forced his body onto and into hers.

Somaly didn't even know that what he was doing to her was called rape. She thought maybe he was cutting her between the legs with a knife. She felt a lightning bolt of pain slicing through her insides. When he was done with her, the merchant said if she spoke about what happened he'd find her and kill her. Grandfather owed him too much, and using her body was the only way he could be repaid.

Then he offered her a piece of candy, as if they were now friends.

Somaly couldn't understand what had just happened, but she knew she felt sick with shame. She ran to the river and jumped in with all her clothes on, begging the water to carry her away.

Even after Somaly figured out that the merchant had raped her, she knew she could not tell anyone. She was too humiliated and scared. She was most scared of Mam Khon and Pen Navy finding out. They were traditional Cambodian people—very quiet and private. Mam Khon had told Somaly that all proper girls should be silent, like the *dam kor*, or silk-cotton tree. She wanted so badly to please her new parents. They would be horrified if they found out who she was now. Somaly knew it wasn't her fault, but she also felt stained and marked for life.

Somaly went back to Grandfather's and he didn't even ask her where the lamp oil was. He just got angry and beat her because she'd come home late. Not that she could feel his blows. All she could feel that night was terror and disgust. And soon after, somewhere in the back of her head, it all clicked into place. Something in the way Grandfather treated her after that day at the merchant's gave him away. She realized Grandfather had sent her to that merchant not for oil, but to be *used*. He sold her virginity to the Chinese merchant to repay his loan.

Somaly stopped talking to Grandfather. She stopped talking to anyone. She didn't know where to turn or how to ask for help. She went to school and did her chores, but it was like she was walking through a fog the whole time. She didn't trust herself to speak without crying. And what could she say even if the words did come out?

According to Cambodian society, once Grandfather took Somaly out of Bou Sra, she was his. Grandfather "owned" Somaly and dictated exactly what she could and could not do. Soon after he used her body to pay off his debt, he made another deal. This time with a soldier named Than.

FICTION: ▬▬▬▬▬▬▬▬▬▬▬▬▬▬▬▬▬▬▬

If you are a man in Cambodia and you sleep with a virgin, you will get new strength and vigor. You will also live longer, you will be protected from AIDS, and your skin will get lighter.

FACT: ▬▬▬▬▬▬▬▬▬▬▬▬▬▬▬▬▬▬▬

Men in Cambodia will pay hundreds or thousands of dollars to rape a virgin for a week because of a virgin's "magical" powers. The brothels today will often sell girls who are five or six years old. After the week is over, the girls are sewn up on the inside so they still look like virgins. Then they can be sold again.

Tamarind Leaves

Grandfather told Somaly to dress in her school uniform. He brought her to a wooden hut with a priest inside. There they made offerings to the ancestral spirits, and the priest announced that Somaly and Than were officially husband and wife. She had never before met Than. He was almost ten years older than she was.

He stood stick-straight like a soldier at attention and only looked at her to bark orders.

He told Somaly that she had to say goodbye to her adoptive family and school because he was taking her many miles away to a village called Chup. Then he flashed his angry eyes at her and dug his sharp fingernails into her skin, so she knew he meant business. Somaly hated him immediately.

Somaly's mother and father could not stop him, even when they saw Somaly in tears. It was like an unwritten law of the land. When a girl was married, she became the husband's "property." Somaly had no choice but to obey.

When Somaly and Than made it to Chup, the first thing Somaly did was try to hatch a plan for running away. But she soon found out there were soldiers hiding everywhere in the fields and plantations around their hut. They all knew Than. They'd rat her out as soon as she stepped foot out of his door.

Than beat her regularly, either because he didn't like the way her hair looked or didn't think she was good at cooking rice. Somaly missed her family and her school so much. She wept all the time, even in front of Than. It didn't matter. He acted like he couldn't see her unless he needed a meal or sex. The only relief she had was when he got an assignment and left her alone. At least then the silence was bearable.

Sometimes he was gone fighting for days or weeks at a time.

While Than was away, Somaly needed money for food, so she started working as a nurse at a nearby medical clinic. The work was grueling and dirty. People came in all the time screaming in pain. They had legs and arms missing from all the land mines planted around Chup. Pregnant ladies came in to give birth, too. Everyone at the clinic tried their best to get the babies out alive and sew up the maimed soldiers, but nobody really knew what they were doing.

The "doctors" were military medics who were guessing most of the time. There was one nurse who took a single class at nursing school. Lots of times, they ran out of medicine and anesthetic. Somaly had to tie the patients down while they operated. She learned how to wash wounds with a dressing of boiled tamarind leaves, water, and salt. Then she said a little prayer and waited to see if the broken patients would live or die.

A lot of them didn't make it. But Somaly wasn't scared of death. She told herself that these corpses were just skin and bones. Not people. That was the only way it made sense.

Somaly felt like she was just skin and bones, too. First Grandfather and the Chinese merchant, then her violent husband Than. Sometimes the men in the clinic who called themselves doctors forced themselves on Somaly, too. All of them grabbed and poked at her body. Now that she was about fifteen and looking more like a woman than a girl, the men pressed and rubbed themselves against her as if playing a game. If she resisted, they would beat her or threaten to tell Than, who would beat her more.

One night the chief doctor raped her and then told her she should be grateful to him because she was too ugly to deserve him. Another doctor, whom Somaly considered a friend, showed her there was no such thing as friendship between a man and a woman.

Somaly had to separate her heart and mind from what they were doing to her physically. She had to tunnel somewhere deep inside while they had their way with her skin and bones. She did this over and over again, squeezing her eyes tightly shut until all she could see was emptiness, until all she could hear was the pulse of her own blood. She climbed into her memories, where she could breathe in the forest air and taste the waterfalls of Bou Sra again. She imagined herself dancing around the harvest fire and swaying in her hammock.

This was how she survived. Her spirit was the one thing these men could never touch.

There was a day though, when Somaly's body frightened her. Than was away fighting when Somaly woke up to see blood flowing from her *secret place*. She had no idea what was happening to her, and she was sure she was cracking in half. She hid at home, waiting for the blood to stop.

When she went back to the clinic for work the next day, the chief nurse screamed at Somaly and demanded an excuse. Somaly had to tell her the truth. The nurse explained that the secret-place blood was her period. This meant soon it would be Somaly's honor to make children for her husband. Then she gave Somaly cloth bandages from the supply closet to put in her underwear and told her she was a real woman now.

Somaly thanked her. But inside she was screaming with new fear and shame. Her body was truly not hers anymore.

> **"**
> ━━━━━━━━━━━━━━━━
>
> *I believe in reality. Only you can drive your life and make decisions on how you want yourself to be.*
>
> ━━━━━━━━━━━ **"**
>
> ~Somaly Mam

Untouched and Untouchable

One day, Than left for a battle along the border. He was supposed to come back in a few days. The days turned into weeks … then a month. Somaly was pretty sure he was dead. There was no part of her that was sad he was gone, but she also didn't know where she could go to live safely on her own.

Grandfather showed up at her door with a "solution."

He told Somaly to pack her bag. They were going to the capital, Phnom Penh. Phnom Penh was wild and noisy compared with the tiny villages and forests where Somaly had lived. Instead of walking paths and huts made of leaves, there were "roads" made of mud, stones, and garbage. There were also rickety buildings, huge open-air markets, and nightclubs.

Grandfather brought Somaly to a woman named Aunty Nop. She lived in a filthy apartment off the central market. Aunty Nop had a wide, pudgy face covered in makeup so thick and bright it looked like a Halloween mask. Somaly couldn't tell if the woman was supposed to be a demon or a geisha doll. Aunty Nop scowled at Somaly and then talked to Grandfather in mumbles before he left.

Aunty Nop told Somaly to put on a special dress and clunky shoes. Then she smeared Somaly's face with the same white, pasty makeup as she used, so Somaly looked like a geisha-demon, too. They walked through a maze of dark alleys to another building that was rotting from the inside out. There were two floors with a cooking pit and sleeping pallets made of grass and dirt. On each pallet was another girl putting on the exact same mask and costume. Even though most of the girls' dresses were made of silk, they pulled them on slowly, like they were made of lead.

Somaly couldn't get enough air to breathe. She knew already that there was something very wrong in this horrible place. Stocky armed guards were posted by the door. The huge room stank of sweat and sadness. The girls on the grass pallets didn't even look up at Somaly as another woman, named Aunty Peuve, showed her around. Everyone looked so tired and small.

Aunty Peuve had a short conference with Aunty Nop. Then she took Somaly to a little private room in the back. (Private because there were a few scarves strung up to keep this corner separate.) Aunty Peuve said she was going to bring Somaly her first client. Somaly knew exactly what was going on now, but she also couldn't let it be true. She thought the walls would come crashing down on her. Maybe the sky, too.

Actually, she *longed* for that to happen. But it didn't.

One of the girls warned Somaly that she'd better do as she was told or she'd be beaten senseless.

Somaly told Aunty Peuve that she refused to have sex with anyone. Aunty Peuve slapped her and brought the man in anyway. Somaly stood in front of him, shaking. Every inch of her skin felt like it was on fire. There were no windows. No doors except the one flanked with guards. Nothing but this horrifying moment where the world was spinning so fast she couldn't see straight, and there was no way to stop this man from coming toward her.

Somaly tried. She definitely tried. She fought that first man mightily. He was tall and strong. She was like a pinned butterfly, struggling to break free and fly away, but caught in his grip. When she was bruised and bloody from his fists, he raped her. Then, to prove he was still in charge and she was utterly helpless, he raped her a second time.

The next night was even worse. Aunty Peuve was furious at Somaly for causing so much trouble. She said Grandfather owed a lot of money and it was up to Somaly to pay off his debt. So Aunty Peuve sent three burly men to use and abuse Somaly's body however they wished. Each of them was more ferocious than the last. One of the men beat Somaly with a belt buckle and a crutch before forcing his way inside her. She later found out that he was actually Aunty Peuve's husband.

But marriage meant nothing. Love meant nothing. The only reason why men came into Aunty Peuve's hellhole was to grab a young girl and molest her any way he wanted. Then the girls were thrown back on their pallets, limp and lifeless. Their painted-doll faces made it even easier for the men to toss them around like toys.

After night two, just to show her who was boss, Aunty Peuve took Somaly down to a cellar that was filled with snakes, scorpions, and sewage. They tied her up and poured snakes all over her. Somaly screamed and cried for hours. She was loud—louder than she'd ever been before. Not because she was scared, but because she was enraged. She didn't know how or why there was an entire planet of people walking, eating, and dreaming, and not one of them could save her.

How was it possible that she was here? Who were these aunties, and since when did Grandfather "owe" them something? And why did Somaly have to pay this cruel man's debts with her life?

When Somaly was released from the punishment room, the same girl who'd warned Somaly the first night found her again. She slowly wiped Somaly's wounds with peroxide. It was the first gentle touch Somaly had felt in years.

Isn't there some way out? Somaly longed to ask the girl. But the girl's lips were shut tight. When she was done wiping away the blood and sewage from Somaly, she walked away. Then she started putting on her white face paint again. Silently.

Whether she wanted to or not, Somaly fell into a kind of routine and learned the ropes. Aunty Peuve and Aunty Nop were *meebons*. That meant they were in charge of feeding, clothing, and housing the girls during the day. Every night the *meebons* rented out the girls to whoever came by. Somaly had no choice but to obey if she wanted to stay alive. Most nights, she wondered if she *did* want to stay alive in a world like this.

Life at the brothel meant that each night Somaly had to have sex with a new lineup of angry, heartless men: soldiers, shopkeepers, truck drivers, even policemen. The soldiers were definitely the fiercest. They threw Somaly around like a rag doll. Sometimes she was forced to go to the central market and have sex with taxi drivers. The taxi drivers rented wooden planks and lined them up on the sidewalk, so people walking past could see them with Somaly. She felt so horribly degraded with every footstep she heard going by.

Other times she was sent away with businessmen for the night. Most of the time these were Chinese men who had a lot of money or a lot of friends. They would throw parties with ten or twenty of their pals. They would pass Somaly around like a bottle of wine, and she couldn't leave until she gave them each pleasure.

When daylight came, Somaly tried desperately to purify her body. Smelling the stink of these men was the worst torture of all. There was no soap at the brothel, so she boiled tamarind leaves in salt water and dressed her wounds just like she'd done for the soldiers back in Chup. It wasn't that she cared about the scars on her skin so much. She just wanted so badly to feel clean, to wash away everything that happened the night before, hoping for a new today.

After she soaked her skin in the tamarind water, Somaly slept in fitful nightmares. If she earned enough, the aunties fed her a bowl of rice when she woke up.

And then it was time to start all over again.

Somaly decided that in order to survive she had to pretend she was a magician. Every night at dusk, while she stirred together the coconut oil and white powder for her face, she imagined that she was turning into a wide, snowy plain. Or a mountain peak so high it kissed the sky. Untouched and untouchable.

She took her time, scooping out the gluey paste and spreading it on her cheeks. Then she drew on dark eyes, rosy cheeks, red lips. By the time the clients came in, she looked like an entirely different being. She closed her eyes forcefully. She shut out the world and left her body. She pictured herself drifting into a sea of white nothingness ... disappearing completely.

> **❝**
>
> *For myself it was too late. I felt like I had died. I had no idea where to go. My life was in darkness.*
>
> **❞**
>
> ~ Somaly Mam

I Was Once You

Somaly lived at the brothel for three brutal years. It wasn't exactly "living." It was numbing her body and her mind, again and again. Most of her waking hours felt helpless, hopeless, and bleak.

Somaly tried to run away from the *meebons*. A few times there were clients who promised to marry her and get her out of the system. But they were all liars. Each time she tried to flee, she was caught and tortured. After a while, she stopped plotting her escapes and just prayed for the morning, when she could boil more tamarind leaves to cleanse her body and try to sleep.

When the *meebons* discovered that Somaly was good at cleaning, they made her do some of the housework, too. They were kind to Somaly as long as she followed their orders. Over time, they even trusted her to stay alone in the house or to take care of the younger girls.

Every time a new girl was brought in, Somaly felt like she was dying a little bit more. Some girls already knew what was happening, but a lot of them walked in completely unaware. A "long-lost uncle" promised to take them to school. Or a "family friend" swore she knew of an easy way to make money. The worst was when girls were brought in by their own parents who sold them to Aunty Peuve for a small wad of cash—right in front of their faces.

How can you do this?! Somaly wanted to scream. But she knew it wouldn't help to say any of this out loud. She tried always to give the new girls a gentle smile and sterilize their fresh cuts and bruises after their first night behind the scarves. That was all she *could* do.

Or was it?

There was something about those two new girls. They were a few years younger than Somaly, maybe thirteen or fourteen. Their hair was dark and shiny, laughing down their backs like hers used to do, too. Somaly watched as Aunty Peuve shoved them into a corner and tied them to a wooden pillar with wet rags.

Somaly felt like she was watching her younger self being led into this hell. Everything about their darting looks and untouched skin seemed so hopeful and desperate at the same time. They still smelled like soap and innocence. Seeing them tied up in the corner made Somaly wince like her whole body was knotted with pain. It was like rewinding her life ... but maybe with the chance to play out a new ending.

She had given up on saving herself. She already felt dead inside. But she couldn't take her eyes off those two girls huddled together. She couldn't sit still and watch this happen to someone else again.

She knew she'd be punished. Her skin was already stinging with the memory of her last lashing. She could envision the snakes in the cellar without even closing her eyes. But she was done being trapped by fear. She stared at the new girls' long hair and still-bright eyes. They had no idea how dark and hellish this existence could be.

Somaly was their only way out.

She had to be stealthy and smart. She waited until Aunty Peuve left to run errands. There was little light inside, but she guessed it was midday because there were no customers and only one guard by the staircase. Somaly knew this guard; he was fat and lazy and usually drunk on rice wine. Somaly stared at him out of the corner of her eye until he melted into a heavy, snoring sleep. Then she crawled over to the new girls without making a sound. She was quieter than a stone. It was like she'd practiced for this moment for the past three years, locking away all her words and emotions and sculpting her body into a shadow.

The girls were crouching and trembling now. There were no windows, of course, but through the cracks of straw and soot walls she could see their wet cheeks. Tears, because they were new. And also because they *knew*.

She found their wrists, tied tightly to a wooden pillar. How many times had Somaly wished the wood would just rot completely and crumble so they could all flee?

She worked quickly and precisely, kneading the rags apart, tugging with her teeth, even. Aunty Peuve had bound them fiercely. The cloths were wet and cold. The girls whimpered while Somaly slogged away. She pulled and clawed with a strength she didn't even know she had. Finally they were both cut loose.

She couldn't let the girls stop to thank her. She just got on her knees and crawled toward the door. They followed her past the rotting grass pallets. Past the cooking hole. Past the broken stairwell.

The guard was still passed out and drooling as they crept by. The alley below was deserted. It reeked of garbage and human waste. Nobody ever came here before dusk. Nobody even knew it existed besides men demanding sex.

Somaly saw the girls' faces for one fleeting moment. Their skin was lighter than hers. Their eyes were wide and frightened. Their mouths were trembling and wanting to ask *why, how, where?*

Somaly said exactly three words: "Don't stay here."

They clutched each other's hand and started running. She watched their skirts skimming over the broken ground, the puddles splashing as they darted between buildings.

Somaly knew she was once just like them. And now, thanks to her, their lives had become possible again.

The *meebons* figured out what had happened as soon as they came back. Somaly was dragged downstairs and punished severely, but no abuse could take away her feeling of victory. She knew she'd done right by those two new girls.

For days afterward, with every crack of the whip and every hour in the snake cellar, Somaly thought of their skirts and their bare feet underneath, sprinting to freedom.

FICTION:

Girls who work in the sex industry are there because they like it. They get treated to fancy clothes and cell phones from their pimps.

FACT:

Most girls in the sex industry are forced in by family, kidnappers, and rapists. It's hard to measure because trafficking is so secretive, but UNICEF (a worldwide organization that defends the rights of children) estimates 1.2 million children are trafficked every year.

A Way Out

Business was slowing down at the brothel. Aunty Peuve made Somaly stand on the side of the road leading to the central market more and more to grab men. One night, Somaly saw a Land Cruiser driving slowly by her. It had a sign on it for one of the foreign humanitarian agencies that was sending money and food to Phnom Penh. The man who got out of the car wanted to rent Somaly for the night.

His name was Dietrich, and he offered to take Somaly to a guesthouse to sleep with her. Aunty Peuve agreed as long as he swore to bring her back by morning.

Somaly had never met someone like Dietrich. First of all, he was white and only spoke Swiss German. Somaly spoke Khmer. She didn't understand what he was saying when he offered to buy her some supper. No one who had paid to be with her had ever offered her food. Dietrich wanted to sit with her after supper and chat. He used a lot of wild gestures and laughed. Somaly got the feeling he was trying to make her laugh, too.

Then Dietrich took her back to the guesthouse where he was staying. To Somaly, it was incredibly fancy. Even though she was nineteen years old by now, she'd never seen a mattress or running water. The bed was so soft, she thought she was falling into a sinkhole when she sat down. When Dietrich asked if she wanted to wash up, the only water she saw in the bathroom was in the bottom of the toilet, so she splashed that on her face.

Dietrich turned on the shower for her, and when the water came shooting out of the spigot, Somaly shrieked in fear. Dietrich was patient and explained that the pipes couldn't come after her or hurt her. He also handed her a bar of soap, which was the most delicious thing she'd smelled since the forest she'd called home as a child.

Though that night felt pretty decadent to Somaly, it was still a transaction. No matter how kind Dietrich was, she knew he had paid to use her body.

When Dietrich returned her to the brothel the next day, he handed Aunty Peuve the fifty cents he owed for Somaly's services. Then, when Aunty wasn't looking, he gave Somaly herself twenty dollars. (That is the equivalent of about two thousand dollars today.)

Somaly didn't want to be bought for any amount of money, but she had to admit she was fascinated by this man. He came back and requested Somaly night after night. Within a few weeks, Dietrich asked Somaly if she wanted to become his "special friend." She could live with him in his villa that had a gate, a kitchen, beds, and soap. Dietrich promised to give her spending money and a key so she could come and go whenever she wanted. Somaly knew it wasn't full freedom, since she'd be "his" at night, but it was much better than the alternative of staying at the brothel. So she said yes.

The *meebons* never argued or came after her. Somaly didn't know why. Maybe because after working for three years, she had already paid off Grandfather's debt and then some. She was never allowed to know how much he owed in the first place.

More likely, Aunty Peuve was getting old and cowardly. Her business was going downhill. Her husband was using up all their earnings and abusing all her girls. Besides, Dietrich was a rich, white man, and nobody messed with rich, white men in Cambodia.

After all her grand dreams of how she would escape and all her nightmares of being beaten to death, Somaly walked out of the aunties' brothel in full daylight, on her own two feet. She began her new life on a day like any other. The sun rose and set like it always did. Only this time, Somaly got to see it with her eyes wide open.

66

The sky is clear after raining.

99

~ Somaly Mam

Love and Other Mysteries

Every day Somaly spent in Dietrich's villa, she felt like she was living in a palace. Each hot shower was another miracle. Only she still had to have sex with Dietrich whenever he wanted. She could never forget that he'd bought her companionship. She was always his "special friend," not living on her own terms. She also felt like she couldn't trust him entirely.

After about six months of living together, Dietrich said he had to go back to Switzerland for work. He really wanted Somaly to come with him. Somaly was not into that idea at all. She was scared because she wouldn't know anyone or speak the language. What if Dietrich turned on her and tried to sell her? That's what had happened every other time she'd trusted a man.

When Somaly said no, Dietrich was disappointed, but he understood. Before he left, he gave her the equivalent of $100,000. He made sure his translator was clear when he said good-bye. He wanted Somaly to use this money to get a motorbike, go to school, anything she wanted. Dietrich was a compassionate man.

The first thing Somaly did with her money was give each of the girls at Aunty Peuve's enough to pay off their "debts" and buy their freedom. Then she enrolled herself at the Alliance Francaise so she could learn French. Dietrich's friend Guillaume gave her a place to stay and helped find her work as a maid. Those first days of independence were thrilling for Somaly. She was so excited to be earning money and living on her own in Cambodia. She had to pinch herself to believe it was true.

At the same time, it was pretty terrifying being on her own. Guillaume invited her to a lot of parties. Somaly liked meeting Guillaume's friends, though she felt like she'd forgotten how to talk—especially with men. She had been told for so long to be silent like the silk-cotton tree. Girls were *property*, not people. Now even introducing herself made her confused and frightened. It was so strange to say *I am Somaly* without adding *I belong to* ... .

Plus, she kept thinking anyone who started talking to her just wanted sex, or worse, to own her, too. At one of Guillaume's parties in 1991, Somaly met a Frenchman named Pierre. Pierre was working for a French relief agency. He was scruffy but handsome. He spoke perfect Khmer, which was huge to Somaly. She hadn't heard a man speak kindly to her in Khmer since she was in that open-air schoolhouse with Mam Khon a lifetime ago. The first night Somaly met Pierre, they talked in Khmer until the early morning.

Pierre was the first man who showed Somaly true respect. He was the first man who took her out just to *be* with her, instead of for sex. He asked her questions and really wanted to hear her answers. Somaly told him her whole story, how she wanted to feel clean and whole again. Pierre was the first man to listen to her dreams and help her make a plan for the future.

Somaly wanted to start a small business. Pierre gave her some funds, and she took them straight to the market to buy school supplies for her family in Thlok Chhrov. With the rest of his wages, Pierre started a café where Somaly and he could work together.

It was clear that Pierre was in love with Somaly and wanted to marry her. She had to tell him she liked him a lot, but she wasn't interested in some great romance. She didn't really believe in the word *love*. She admired him and was grateful for their new life together. But she couldn't be married to him or anyone else for that matter. It brought back too many nightmares of Than. Pierre said he could appreciate that.

The café did well for the first year or so. Phnom Penh was bustling at the time. The prince had just returned to power and the Vietnamese occupation was over. The United Nations sent in 22,000 peacekeepers to help the government transition. All this meant there was a lot of new money and thirsty foreigners to stop by the café.

Sadly, it also meant the brothel business was getting busier in Phnom Penh, too. Every day, lots of new restaurants and bars were opening up. They served food and after-dinner "entertainment" from young women. Pierre made sure that any man who came into his café with a girl who looked underage was thrown out immediately. Somaly saw Pierre fly into a rage more than once. He had a bad temper. It made him lose a lot of business, but he didn't care. Pierre was a man of principles.

Somaly made a small but steady income as a waitress in the café. Every time she got paid, she brought more food and school supplies back to her family in Thlok Chhrov. They were still struggling just to feed themselves. No matter who was in power, the government was completely out of touch with what was going on in the countryside. There were many people starving to death or selling their daughters for bags of rice.

About a year after opening the café, Pierre told Somaly that they'd lost too much money. He needed to cut his losses and close up shop. He asked Somaly again to marry him. His new plan was for them to settle down in France. Even though they'd been a couple for a long time, Somaly still didn't want to attach herself to any man. She really struggled with the thought of being bound to Pierre in any legal way.

Still, the café was shutting down. Most of the Cambodians Somaly knew were trying to get out of the country as fast as possible. The United Nations was organizing the first government elections, and people said it would lead to another war. Everyone Somaly talked to said that if she had the opportunity to leave, she should.

In order for her to get a passport and visa, Somaly and Pierre had to be married. Pierre pleaded with her over and over again until Somaly finally said okay. They went to the French embassy and signed all the papers. It was the first time Somaly ever wrote her name on an official document. She didn't know her date of birth. She had to make it up.

She took Pierre back to Thlok Chhrov so they could say goodbye to her adoptive family. Her father was very worried about her leaving. Her mother begged

Pierre not to abuse Somaly. They'd seen this happen with their other daughters. Marriage in Cambodia still meant the husband could do whatever he wanted to his wife because he *owned* her.

Somaly tried to explain that Pierre was French and had a good heart. But inside, she couldn't shake the feeling that one day he would turn around and try to sell her, too. She swore to Pierre and to her parents that she would be back soon. Then, before boarding the plane, Somaly packed a sharp knife in her suitcase, just in case Pierre tried anything funny. If she was going to start a new life, she was going to do it on her own terms.

> *Life is never over; you can turn your life's page. You will never forget it but you can forgive. Don't be afraid to start a new life again and again.*
>
> ~ Somaly Mam

Unspoken Promise

France was like a completely different universe to Somaly. Pierre's family seemed loud and rude to her. Plus, she couldn't get over how much food was wasted at every meal. She could feed an entire family in Cambodia—for a week—with the crusts of bread left after breakfast.

But Somaly was determined to give France a try. She was ready to start from scratch, even if that meant throwing away platefuls of untouched food and smiling when Pierre's mom insulted her (which she did a lot).

Somaly started studying children's books and newspapers, so she could learn more French. She answered an ad and got a job as a maid in a hotel. Most of the people staying at the hotel were very old. None of the other maids paid attention to them. But Somaly had been taught always to respect and care for the elderly. She thought the residents were sweet and lonely. After cleaning rooms and waiting tables, she started visiting a few and rubbing their feet. They taught her French and called her beautiful. They also gave her lots of tips.

While Pierre was still looking for work, Somaly earned 2,500 francs in two months. This was enough for them to rent a one-bedroom apartment in Nice. Somaly felt really proud of herself and of her new earnings. She started working nights at a restaurant, too. Then she added a third job of harvesting grapes in the countryside.

Everyone who met Somaly was amazed by her strength and strong work ethic. She slept about four hours a night and still woke up full of momentum. (Not to mention, she could easily crush more grapes than Pierre.) She was so happy to get praised for her new skills.

She was now more than just a body. She had a keen mind and a generous heart. She really was her own person.

After a year and a half in Nice, Pierre got an assignment back in Cambodia. It was with *Medecins Sans Frontieres* (Doctors Without Borders, a humanitarian agency giving medical services to countries in crisis). Somaly was a little sad to be leaving, but she also wanted to get back to her homeland. She felt exhilarated by how much she'd learned and grown in the short time she'd been away. She was ready to return to Cambodia with a new confidence. She could look people directly in the eye now and express herself clearly. Most of all, she knew there were girls in Cambodia who never had this sense of self-worth. Somaly was determined to change that.

Somaly and Pierre moved into a house about two hundred miles north of Phnom Penh, in a town called Kratie. They lived with fellow workers from Medecins Sans Frontieres (MSF). Somaly started volunteering at the MSF clinic as a translator and medical assistant. She worked with the doctors who treated sexually transmitted diseases. Most of her patients were men. She knew these were the same men who were going to the brothels or paying for sex on the side of the road. They were infecting countless young women every night.

Somaly hated who they were and what they did. She also knew she had to care for them if she was ever going to change the cycle of abuse and disease.

One day at the MSF clinic, an eighteen-year-old girl came in. Somaly could tell she was caught in the sex trade, but she didn't want to ask. That would only embarrass or scare the girl away. Instead, Somaly gently explained the risks of infection and showed the girl how to use condoms. It was 1994. AIDS had just come to Cambodia and it was getting more and more people sick.

Before saying good-bye, Somaly asked her patient to tell her friends to come to the MSF clinic for treatment. Somaly promised she would be there every morning and would personally make sure they were cared for kindly.

The girls started filing in each morning. No questions asked, no judgments or scorn. Somaly gave each girl medicine and condoms. She also made sure to give them a look that said *I get it*.

Soon, Somaly didn't wait for the girls to come into the clinic. She went directly to the brothels themselves. She asked Pierre's boss if she could have a stock of condoms and soap so she could pass them out as she worked her way through the alleys. Pierre's boss wanted to help her, but it was hard to get MSF to foot the bill for hundreds of bars of soap. They were supposed to be giving out only medicine.

Somaly didn't waste time fighting. She knew, once again, that nobody took the situation in the brothels seriously. Nobody saw how endangered these girls were. Pierre's boss handed her some boxes of condoms. Somaly emptied her pockets, marched down to the market, and bought the soap herself.

Walking back into a brothel for the first time was horrible in a thousand ways. Somaly was sure she'd break down seeing the girls on the floor, helpless and alone. The thing was, she couldn't show a sliver of emotion if she wanted to be taken seriously. So she dressed up as an official nurse, sucked in her breath, and held her head up high.

She told the pasty-faced *meebons* that she was the wife of a white foreigner and that it was in the best interests of the brothel for the girls to stay healthy. She showed them her stash of condoms and soap. They were impressed with her status. They also wanted their girls to be hearty so they could bring in more money. So, they let her in. Soon, they even let Somaly bring some of the sicker girls to the clinic for medical care.

Somaly loved being able to wash and feed these girls at the clinic.

She hated promising to get them back in time for work each night.

Spending time in the brothels of Kratie was the hardest, most invigorating work Somaly had ever done. She was so grateful for every girl she met. This was where Somaly belonged. She knew it in her gut. And yet, there was so much more she wanted to do for them besides hand them a box of condoms and some soap.

She made an unspoken promise to each and every young woman. She would get them out if it was the last thing she did.

> **" **Life is life. You were born alone, you can die alone, but how will you manage your life? I prefer to die for good causes. **"**

~ Somaly Mam

Finding Her Cause

Somaly's plan started with one girl. She was sixteen years old with dark skin and pin-straight hair. It wasn't that she was incurably sick or broken in any new way. It was just impossible for Somaly to watch another girl be held captive in this brutal system.

Somaly talked to one of the Kratie *meebons* and told her the girl needed to come to the clinic for care. Then she told the girl to meet her in a secret location instead of coming to the clinic.

Somaly got a car from MSF and drove the girl to a village about ten miles away. In the village lived a seamstress. Somaly had already paid her $100. In return, the seamstress promised to take in the girl and train her in sewing, which would hopefully lead her to a job and a way to live on her own.

One hundred dollars was a lot of money in Cambodia in the late nineties. Somaly just prayed it was enough to buy this girl's escape route.

When the *meebon* came looking for the girl at the MSF clinic, the doctors and nurses swore she had never shown up. Somaly was already back from her mission and shrugged her shoulders, too, as if to say *Sorry, the girl must've fled.*

After it worked with the first girl, Somaly did it with another two. And then two more. She had to be clever and selective. She picked girls from different brothels in different parts of town. That way she left no trail behind.

The seamstress turned out to be an incredible ally. She was true to her word and took good care of Somaly's escapees. But Somaly could never visit them. And once they left the seamstress for their new lives, Somaly had no idea where they went, whether they made it on their own or got yanked back into the nightmare of trafficking.

She wished more than anything that she could take in all these girls somehow. She wanted to build a safe house where the pimps and *meebons* couldn't find them. She started mapping out exactly what this would look like, how much funding it would take, and how many cots she could fit side by side on the floor. She needed to get more seamstresses and sewing machines, too, so the girls could be taught a marketable skill. It was about more than just pulling them out of the brothels. Somaly knew that if she were really going to help them survive, she needed to give them a chance to start over, to earn an income, to see themselves as new and empowered.

Pierre and one of his colleagues from MSF started writing a charter to collect funds for Somaly's survivor-empowerment project. Then, two unexpected things happened: Pierre got another job with an American relief agency and had to move back to Phnom Penh, and Somaly realized she was pregnant.

> **❝** [My children] have to feel beloved. **❞**

~ Somaly Mam

Little Flowers

Somaly was not thrilled about having a baby. She thought children were too vulnerable. Every day she was hearing about more and more little girls being kidnapped or enslaved. How would she ever protect this new being? She watched her belly start to grow. She had to figure it out, and soon.

Somaly and Pierre moved to a neighborhood just outside of Phnom Penh that turned out to be full of brothels. There was a street near their home called *La Rue des Petites Fleurs* (The Street of Little Flowers). Somaly knew that meant it was full of young girls for sale.

She began each morning making her rounds to the brothels. She gave out condoms and took girls into the nearby clinic. The alleys of Phnom Penh were all too familiar. It was so painful and surreal to be retracing her own footsteps, breathing in mountains of garbage, and hearing the *meebons* screeching.

But Somaly knew she had to charge through the tornado of gruesome memories. Every time she felt like turning around, she looked up to see more girls' painted faces peeking out of shacks. She could not ignore those white painted cheeks and stained lips.

She knocked on each door firmly. She told the *meebons* she was a health worker for MSF. Even though that wasn't exactly true anymore, Somaly didn't care. She was done playing by the rules.

Meanwhile, Somaly's family was expanding by the minute. One of her adopted sisters from Thlok Chhrov, Phanna, came to Somaly and admitted tearfully that her husband wanted to sell their daughter Ning. Phanna was desperate to save her. She was also too scared to disobey her violent husband. Somaly was eight months pregnant, but it wasn't even a choice for her. She told Phanna that from now on, Ning would live safely with her and Pierre. And so her five-year-old niece moved in and soon became a daughter to Somaly.

In 1995, Somaly gave birth to a beautiful little girl named Adana. The moment she became a mother, Somaly felt her world open up with hope and possibility. All of her fears melted away when she hugged

Adana in her arms. Those new, trusting eyes looked back at her with pure love. Somaly swore to Adana that she would always keep her safe.

Soon after Adana's birth, Somaly got a knock on the door from a man named Robert Deutsch. Robert ran an American relief agency and needed help because a mother from the village was sure her daughter had been sold into a brothel. The girl's name was Srey. She'd been tricked by a family friend. Robert respected Somaly's commitment to her cause and promised they'd work as a team to save Srey.

Somaly found a police officer whom she trusted. She had him go into the brothel disguised as a client and ask for Srey. The *meebons* told him Srey was too sick to serve anybody. So Somaly and Robert gathered a few more policemen and tried to stage their first brothel raid.

It wasn't exactly a success. The pimps were forcing the girls out the back door while Somaly and her team came through the front. But they did manage to rescue Srey, who was delirious and nearly unconscious. Somaly handed her back to her mother and they filed charges at the police station. They all felt at least a little triumphant.

The only thing was, the pimps had gotten Srey addicted to heavy drugs to keep her obedient. When Srey got home and started detoxing, she got very sick.

Srey's mom told Somaly that she couldn't handle this howling animal that used to be her daughter. Then she basically left Srey on Somaly's doorstep.

Somaly took her in and told Srey it would all start getting better now.

FICTION: ▰▰▰▰▰▰▰▰▰▰▰▰▰▰

Pimps and traffickers protect the girls they bring into the sex trade and share whatever money is earned.

FACT: ▰▰▰▰▰▰▰▰▰▰▰▰▰▰▰▰▰▰

Pimps and traffickers offer no protection and rarely share a single cent. Instead, they make their victims earn a certain amount (quota) each night, and if that amount isn't made, the victims suffer severe beatings.

Ready to Fly

Somaly never thought she'd run a shelter out of her home, but that's what happened. After Srey came to live with them, it felt impossible to close the door on the next girl, or the one after that.

Meanwhile, Somaly had a newborn baby to take care of. Some of the girls Somaly took in were pregnant, too, or they brought their young children with them. Pierre wasn't making that much money at his relief agency. The house where she and Pierre lived had two bedrooms and a living room. It was getting very crowded. And there were a lot of mouths to feed.

Somaly got a job in real estate, mostly so she could look for a bigger home just for the rescued girls.

Pierre and his friend finished the charter for Somaly's charity project. She called her organization AFESIP. In French, it stands for *Agir Pour les Femmes en Situation Précaire*, or in English, Acting for Women in Distressing Situations. Somaly marched the charter down to the offices of the European Union (a group of European countries). They had a representative in Phnom Penh.

Somaly explained they needed more space, some beds, and sewing machines. The representative asked why. Somaly said there were thousands of victims of sexual exploitation who needed to be rescued. They needed a safe place to stay where they could learn new skills to start over. The people at the European Union office just shrugged and said they didn't think there was a problem with forced prostitution.

Somaly wanted to shake them and slap them silly, though she knew that would never help her get the money she needed. So she filed her application for funds and walked out. It was like throwing all of her hopes into the wind.

It took months of arguing her case and pleading. She spoke to anyone and everyone who would listen. Meanwhile, her house was getting fuller and more chaotic every day. One night, Pierre said he couldn't take it anymore. He told Somaly that she had to find a new place for all the girls to stay, or he would throw them out on the street.

Save the Children UK was the first organization to send a helping hand. They offered Somaly a one-room house on stilts. It had just enough room to lay out the girls' mats on the floor for sleeping. Then PADEK (the anti-poverty organization that helped rescue Srey) donated $6,000 in starter funds. Somaly was so relieved she felt like she had just sprouted wings.

And she was ready to fly.

The scars on her skin and the nightmares that still haunted her each night—they'd all led Somaly here, to this moment. As she lay those mats down, she thought about all the new dreams these girls would make together. She felt like she was buzzing with purpose and promise.

She also knew she needed more than beds and sewing machines to make her center feel safe and bright. She couldn't be there around the clock. She wanted a trusted soul to live there with the rescued girls, someone who would be compassionate and nurturing. But, who?

Then she thought of the perfect answer. She went back to Thlok Chhrov and asked her adoptive mother, Pen Navy. Her mother was crying as she said *Yes, of course.* Somaly also got one of her adoptive sisters to teach the girls sewing. They lined up the sewing machines under the stilts of the house. The hum of stitching was like an engine fueling their spirits, vibrating in the floorboards, pushing them into their futures.

AFESIP officially opened its doors on March 8, 1997. Somaly didn't want to draw too much attention. After all, the girls were escapees and could still be caught. But Somaly did invite some government officials whom she admired. It was the first time she stood up and claimed her lifelong dream to be not only a survivor, but also an advocate.

AFESIP was here to help all endangered women. Holding her daughter, Adana, and thanking her guests and survivors, Somaly couldn't have been prouder.

66 ▬▬▬▬▬▬▬▬▬▬▬▬▬▬▬▬▬▬▬

It is not about strength, it is about we should do what we can.

▬▬▬▬▬▬▬▬▬▬▬▬▬ 99

~ Somaly Mam

Saying It Out Loud

It wasn't all clear skies once AFESIP opened, though. And while she was getting support from overseas, Somaly was definitely playing a tricky game in Cambodia. She was getting recognized more and more in the streets. She started getting threats from pimps. They all said the same thing: If she didn't stop helping girls break out of the brothels, she'd be killed.

Somaly couldn't exactly turn to the police for protection. A lot of the officers went to the brothels for sex, too. Or sometimes the pimps paid them to keep quiet. One day in the market, a man on a motorbike put a gun in Somaly's side and told her that her days were numbered. Then her parents' house back in Thlok Chhrov was torched. Blessedly, nobody was inside.

Still, the message was loud and clear. Somaly and her family were not safe. Pierre demanded that she take a break and told her they were going on a trip. She hired a bodyguard and the whole family went to Laos, a country north of Cambodia, for a little while. Before they left, Somaly wrote a letter to the prime minister of Cambodia to see if he could help her cause. She knew he'd never get the letter. It was like putting a note in a bottle and casting it out to sea. And yet, where else could she turn?

It was hard for Somaly to be away from all the young women of AFESIP, even though she knew they were in good hands with her adoptive mother in charge. Somaly loved being a mother to Adana and Ning. She also felt like she was mother, sister, and mentor to these newly freed girls. She was so frustrated and furious that thugs were stopping her work. Pierre was getting pretty exasperated about all the commotion in their lives, too. The trip to Laos was a respite, but it also made them all pretty anxious. They just wanted to get back home as soon as possible.

When the prime minister of Cambodia replied to Somaly's letter, she couldn't believe her eyes. He promised to investigate the burning of her parents' house. He also wrote that he believed in her work. He knew there was a real problem with trafficking. He wanted her back in Cambodia. And so, Somaly returned.

Soon after she came back, AFESIP got funds from the European Union and UNICEF. Somaly went straight to work setting up another shelter outside of Phnom Penh. AFESIP's one-room house was overstuffed with women and children. The new space would have room for several bedrooms, a classroom where the women could learn literacy and basic math, and another room for sewing classes.

Then Somaly got a humanitarian award from the Prince of Asturias in Spain. She and her family flew to Spain in first class. She had to speak in front of royalty and Nobel Peace Prize winners, and she was sure she would melt into a puddle of nerves. But she stood up on the stage and spoke about what it was like to be a Cambodian girl. What it was like to paint on a doll's face every night and tunnel inside while the men used her body any way they wished. What it was like to see so many girls just like her.

The wild applause after Somaly's speech filled her whole body with electricity. People were crying and cheering. She got to meet the prince and queen of Spain. They thanked her for her dedication and vision. Mobs of people asked for Somaly's autograph.

Somaly couldn't believe she could talk about her darkest past in front of these people and still be respected. She always thought it was her fault that she'd been sold into slavery and that she should be ashamed of what she'd done with her body.

But that day in Spain, saying it out loud, in front of this huge crowd, was a huge turning point for Somaly. She got new perspective about her mission and herself. She had been sold into servitude and treated cruelly because sex trafficking was silently accepted—not because of anything Somaly wanted or deserved.

Now she was claiming her past so she could move proudly into her present and future. She was meant to tell her story to the world. She was the only one who knew it from the inside out, the only one who could speak for all the girls still imprisoned.

With the money from Spain, Somaly finished the new shelter. Then she started on a home specifically for the little children who'd been rescued. She found some land near her parents' old home in Thlok Chhrov, Kampong Cham Province. She built a house with a fish pond, a chicken coop, sewing machines, and weaving looms. The kids could learn how to farm or just run in the tall grasses. Best of all, Somaly's adoptive father, Mam Khon, still taught at the village schoolhouse, and she showed her house full of young girls the crisp new uniforms they could wear with pride. She told the girls how long and hard she'd begged Grandfather for the chance to wear that same blue skirt and white shirt. How she'd washed it in the very same river.

This is how she got those little girls to trust her. Many of them were so young and frightened that they didn't smile for months and they didn't talk for years after she found and rescued them. But Somaly walked them through Thlok Chhrov and introduced them to the fields and the sky. Even though it was heartbreaking to see how young they were when they were abused, Somaly was exhilarated knowing they could begin their lives again.

Slowly, the girls started hearing her and hoping with her. Somaly felt proudest of all about the Kampong Cham center. Here she saw twelve- and fifteen-year-olds holding one another's hands and weaving side by side. They called one another "sister." The older girls helped the younger ones with schoolwork. They became the family they'd always wanted, and never had.

66 ▰▰▰▰▰▰▰▰▰▰▰▰▰

No child wants to be a bad luck girl, and the bad luck is not going to touch everyone; even if you have been very badly treated, you can still prove this to them. I always tell my girls not to fight back. In contrast, please remain respectful...the people who are negative are then ashamed and start changing their concept of how we must treat one another.

▰▰▰▰▰▰▰▰ **99**

~ Somaly Mam

Milestones

Police Precinct Offices. Phnom Penh, Cambodia, 1999

Somaly looked out at the crowd of foreign faces—a room full of policemen and soldiers. Every set of eyes looked back at her like she was crazy. Many of the men sneered or openly laughed at her as she spoke.

Then Somaly held up a banana in one hand and a condom in the other. She demonstrated to the men how to put on a condom. There was a lot of squirming from the audience, but not as much laughing anymore. AIDS was sweeping through Cambodia by 1999. Many of the men were scared, although they would never say it out loud.

Somaly started asking questions.

How many of you had your first sexual experience in a brothel?

Why do you enjoy visiting prostitutes?

What exactly gives you sexual pleasure?

It wasn't easy to get the policemen and soldiers to talk. She had brought Mr. Chheng with her. He was a male social worker at AFESIP. He started asking the questions with her. Maybe if the men were too angry or embarrassed to answer her, they could talk to Chheng instead.

Slowly, a few voices started floating back.

Of course I started in a brothel. Where else?

My wife orders *me to go to prostitutes.*

Sexual pleasure…? What is that?

In Cambodian culture, sex was always about male dominance and asserting power. There was no sense of enjoyment for the woman or the man. That's why Somaly wanted to make these presentations. She wasn't there to yell at the men or prove them wrong. She went to the Ministry of Defense in 1999 and said it was time to talk to the men of Cambodia about how they had been indoctrinated, too. Growing up in a world where most boys had their first sexual experiences through rape was a recipe for disaster. She wanted men to know they could change this mentality.

Some of the girls from the AFESIP shelter asked if they could come to Somaly's lectures, too. They wanted to describe what it felt like to be forced into sex. Somaly told them it was a tricky situation and she couldn't promise the men would listen. The girls said they wanted to go anyway.

The response was astounding. A lot of the men wept as they listened to Somaly's survivors. They got four hundred thank-you notes in the first month of starting the program.

Thank you for telling your story.
Thank you for saying this out loud.
Thank you for the incredible work you do.

AFESIP Fair Fashion Offices. Kompong Cham, Cambodia, 2003

This time, the crowd of faces was familiar and cheerful. The girls chatted with one another and shared patterns and ideas in between workstations. Many of them had learned how to sew from Somaly's adopted sister (from the sagging birdhouse in Thlok Chhrov). It was the first thing these survivors could focus on after the horrors of what they had been through. Learning a skill that used their minds and their hands was extremely therapeutic and healing.

Lots of garment factories were airless and had no windows. The workers were paid pennies. But Somaly's Fair Fashion workshop was a ray of light. She looked out at the girls at their tables and felt herself beaming. She had created a safe space where survivors could see their beautiful handwork and sell their crafts.

Most important, everyone in the room wanted to be here. They wanted to thread the bobbin and feel the *ratatatatat* of the machines thrum in their skin. They were in this together. They each shared a common past. And they were each ready for a different future.

Gripsholm Castle. Mariefred, Sweden, 2008

The crowd of faces was bright and loud. Hands of all ages and colors of skin applauded Somaly as she walked to the podium and accepted the World Children's Prize for the Rights of the Child. This was such a momentous occasion for her. Six and a half million children from all over the world voted for Somaly to get the award.

She was not only here *for* them, she was here *because* of them.

***

It wasn't all smooth sailing and award ceremonies, though. As AFESIP grew, there were some heartbreaking setbacks. Botched raids where the police turned out to be working for the pimps. Funding cut off suddenly with no explanation. Some of the rescued women left the AFESIP shelter because they trusted only their traffickers. The scariest obstacles were the recurring threats to Somaly and her family.

She was careful to keep her girls safe. More than once, she had to hire a security team for her family. She also had to close shelters sometimes and build big walls around them when she opened their doors again.

Even so, through the years, AFESIP took its hits and came back ready for the fight. Somaly made sure she sat down with every young girl who walked into an AFESIP shelter. She told them that they could come and get medical treatment and then leave, or stay for as long as they wanted. She told them they were safe, they were loved, they had their whole lives ahead of them.

Somaly was living proof that this was true. That anything was possible.

> ❝ *Life is never ended here in the brothels. Life is in your hand. You can manage it as what you want. The most challenging part is starting new life and forgetting the past.* ❞

~ Somaly Mam

Voices for Change

In 2010, Somaly started a program called Voices for Change. The Voices for Change are girls who were once trafficked or sexually exploited. With Somaly's help, they became survivors.

And now they are change makers.

These young women see firsthand how Somaly fought her way out of her past, how she went from victim to advocate. They've decided they want to become advocates, too. They want to stand up with Somaly and say *This happened to me and it should never happen again.*

Somaly is very clear with the girls who want to join Voices for Change. Advocacy work is not easy.

She doesn't want any of the girls to feel like they have to do it. They often have to face their worst demons by speaking out. Shame. Fear. Reliving nightmares of what can never be undone.

Somaly knows this because she still faces these same demons herself. She is constantly being flown all over the globe to promote her cause and receive awards. She was named one of Vital Voices' Global Leaders and *Time*'s 100 Most Influential People in the World. She's opened shelters in multiple countries, too.

But that does not mean it gets easier to share her story. Even today, each time she begins to speak, the words feel as sharp and close as if she were meeting Grandfather for the first time. She does a lot of meditation and work with a psychologist. Most of all, she learns from the love and courage of the girls she saves.

More than four thousand Cambodian women and another three thousand in Thailand, Laos, and Vietnam owe their freedom to Somaly. Every time she gets up to relay her history, she thinks of them. She hopes she can reach more girls who may be too fearful to come forward themselves, or feel too "dirty" to see their worth.

Voices for Change has new members and momentum every day. Somaly leads by example. Sometimes when Somaly travels for awareness events, she brings young women of the Voices for Change with her. They tell their stories, too. This way people can see that it's real girls, no different than you or me, who are fighting this fight. The future of human rights is now their life's mission.

Back in Cambodia, the Voices for Change help newly rescued girls who come to the shelter, shocked and confused. Voices for Change members guide their new "sisters," filling in the intake forms and holding hands. Many of the girls in Voices for Change get trained to speak with magistrates and judges, too. They go with Somaly to hear court cases against traffickers and help advocate for victims' rights to protect young women.

Each condom brought to a brothel.

Each girl walking into an AFESIP clinic for free medical treatment.

Each court case where a trafficker is convicted— there were thirteen in 2012!

These are the victories of Somaly and her Voices for Change. This is the way we make a new world.

And it all started with one little girl who strung a hammock between two trees in a forest that she called home.

" ▬▬▬▬▬▬▬▬▬▬▬▬

Hope comes true when you see thousands of girls are in your hands and they are smiling. Everyone can't do everything, but each of you can do one thing to end sex slavery. It starts from you today.

▬▬▬▬▬▬▬▬ **"**

~ Somaly Mam

> ❝
> *On my Twitter profile I'm like a list of things. I'm a lover. I'm a friend... an artist. And I don't really want to carry rocks around all the time, but, yeah, I'm a rock collector.*❞
>
> ~ Minh Dang

Rock Collector

The houses on Minh Dang's street all looked a lot alike. This was San Jose, California, in the 1990s. Instead of front lawns or swing sets, many people in her neighborhood had a yard full of white quartz rocks and rosebushes. The neighbors smiled at one another before going in and closing their front doors. Nobody got in anyone else's business or asked too many questions.

Minh spent a lot of time with those rocks in her front yard. They were as bright as stars. Sometimes she pretended they were pieces of the moon or precious gems she could dig up like buried treasure. Minh wasn't allowed to go any farther than her yard to play, so sitting there in that sea of rocks was the only way she could find fun.

When no one was looking, she talked to those rocks, too. She told them they were beautiful and she gave them names. She picked through carefully and filled shoeboxes with her absolute favorites—the ones that were extra sparkly or had a funny-looking zigzag stripe or maybe a side so smooth that it warmed her hand from the California sun. Minh took good care of those rocks. Her collection grew and grew. She hid her shoeboxes in a corner of the garage. She didn't want them to get in the way and make anyone in her house angry.

It was hard for Minh to figure out exactly what made her parents so angry all the time. She worked hard to follow the rules. She got good grades at her public school and was a star on her soccer team. She came home every day and did her homework first thing. She kept her mouth shut. But still, she was always in trouble. Only, her parents never called it trouble. They never called it anything.

It was just part of her day, like sunrise or sunset. Every time Minh climbed into bed, she feared that her father would come for her in the dark. Many nights, from the time she was three old, her father visited her in her bedroom and sexually abused her. With each visit, Minh was overwhelmed with fear and pain. She didn't understand what was happening to her, but she knew it was wrong. If she cried out or said no, he beat her. And when he was finished, Minh's mom came in and beat her anyway. She called Minh horrible names and blamed her for what was happening. She treated Minh like a perpetrator instead of a victim. Like an enemy instead of her child.

Both of her parents made it clear that if Minh said anything to anyone, they would send her away to Vietnam (where they were both born), or kill her.

That's another reason why those rocks in the front yard were so special to Minh. They were really the only things she could talk to. Even if they weren't people, they felt calm and they seemed to listen to her. They were her best friends; her only friends.

Then one day, when Minh was about ten years old, her mom went looking for something in the garage and Minh heard her yell, "What the *#$@ are these doing here?"

Minh tried to run in and save her rocks, but her mom didn't even wait for an answer. She just opened the shoeboxes and scattered the insides all over the yard. It didn't matter that Minh had picked each one and placed them just so. It didn't matter that she'd packed them in rock "families" and knew all their cracks and edges.

Once her mom went back inside, Minh tried to collect the same rocks again. There were thousands to choose from, but she worked as carefully and as quickly as possible, apologizing to the ones she had to leave behind. She raced to get the rock moms and dads and the little rock children reunited before sundown.

That night her dad raped her again. That night her mom beat her again for "making him do it."

But the worst part to Minh was the next day when she came home from school and saw that her shoeboxes were empty again. She ran out to the yard and began digging. She begged the rocks to hold on until she found them. Her fingers got scratched and raw as she searched and searched. Then she frantically crammed the shoeboxes in the garage and scrambled to get her homework done before her dad came for her in the dark.

It kept going like this: Rape. Beat. School. Search. Rape. Beat. School. Search.

And then Minh came home from school one day, saw her empty shoeboxes again, and something in her broke. She tore through the rocks outside. None of them looked familiar or beautiful to her anymore. She was so tired of digging, so confused and lonely and hopeless.

Now it was Minh's turn to get angry.

She threw the empty boxes down and started screaming at the rocks.

"I hate you! I don't need you! You're just stupid, stupid rocks!"

She knew these words so well by now. She was just echoing everything that had been screamed at her before.

FICTION: ████████████████████████████

The sex industry is very secretive. Ladies of the evening stand on street corners or back alleys and proposition people in seedy bars.

FACT: ████████████████████████████████

There are tons of ads in newspapers and on-line that make it clear they're selling sex. Hint: anything that says "barely legal" *isn't legal at all.* Village Voice Media makes an estimated $22 million each year from these ads. Craigslist.com and Backpage.com are also big hotspots for ads. And there are things called "john boards" that list places where people can find commercial sex nearby.

Here's the Deal ...

When Minh turned ten, her father took her to a local café in the Bay area. In the back were private rooms where Minh was told to wait. Soon a man came into Minh's room and raped her. Minh knew this feeling all too well. She felt faceless, nameless, and lifeless, lying under the stranger like a piece of furniture.

As she was getting dressed, Minh heard her father make a deal with the café owner. He promised to bring Minh to this café regularly so people could pay to use her body however they liked. The café/brothel owner would get a percentage for handling the clients, Minh's parents would get the rest. Minh's father told him proudly that she was very obedient.

Minh couldn't feel her legs as she walked out of that back room. She couldn't tell whether it was day or night. All she knew was that she'd just been sold—sold by the two people who were supposed to love, nurture, and protect her from all danger.

Now they were the real danger.

Her father pushed her back into the car. It was almost dawn already. Then he drove her home through the streets of San Jose where other moms and dads were turning on the coffeepot, pouring cereal, or opening the curtains and whispering *good morning* to their slumbering children.

When Minh's father brought her inside, he told her to get in the shower and get ready for school. No one mentioned the deal. Her parents did not even try to explain or apologize. This was her unspoken obligation. Her duty as their daughter.

This was Minh's routine through middle school and high school. She constantly struggled to stay awake in class after countless sleepless nights. Then she went to soccer practice and tried to do some home-work before getting shuttled to the brothel for another eight hours of being raped and beaten. Her life circled around her in a horrible loop, strangling her. Most mornings she saw the dawn as she went home. Some-times her parents didn't even pick her up, but they demanded that Minh get home before sunrise. Then Minh scrubbed her body as if she could wash away the night, got dressed, and started all over again.

The only thing that changed for Minh was that there was a little less screaming in her house now. Her parents were too busy driving Minh back and forth to the brothel and managing all the clients. They placed advertisements in Vietnamese newspapers and maga-zines that stated they had a young girl whose body they were willing to sell. If Minh made a lot of money in one night, her dad took a break from yelling at her. She sometimes even got a smirk from her mom that Minh tried to interpret as a smile.

Minh wished she didn't think of smirks and silence as love.

> **❝**
>
> *I was still a kid who really wanted to hope that her parents could change and that they were good people. So I didn't really want to tell on them. I just couldn't within myself, get over that.*
>
> **❞**
>
> ~ Minh Dang

Questions with No Answers

Minh was having trouble keeping it together at school. She still got A's in all her classes and ran faster than anyone else on the soccer field, but inside she felt like she was unraveling. The sleepless nights and secrets churned in her gut. She was exhausted from hiding all the bruises and scratches and from putting on a calm face when all she could think about was the men who grabbed and groped her each night. More and more, she had to stake out corners in the locker room where she could sob. Sometimes she lost it in the middle of a class and had to pull her hair over her face or run out to the bathroom.

Still, she never breathed a word of what was going on. Even when her teachers asked her why she looked tired and depressed, she buttoned her lips and protected her family. "You know, a lot going on," she might say. Or, "Really busy I guess." Most of the time, whoever was questioning left it at that.

There was a middle school choir teacher, though, who saw Minh's tears and asked her to stay after the bell.

"What's going on?" the choir teacher asked softly.

Minh shrugged and shook her head.

"You can tell me," the teacher said.

Minh whispered her usual response, "Nothing much. Just tired," but the choir teacher wasn't buying it. She just sat there and waited for Minh to say something, anything. Finally, Minh muttered, "My parents are sorta having marital issues." This was actually true. Minh's mom had started threatening to divorce her dad on a regular basis. But Minh never believed she'd do it.

"This is more than divorce issues," Minh's teacher said. That's when the floodgates really opened. Minh bawled and howled. Her whole body ached with the desire to trust this woman and tell her everything. Minh wanted so desperately to be carried away from this room, this life, this reality. Maybe she could leave the country with her teacher, and they could change their faces and fingerprints and truly start over.

But Minh was too smart to believe even her own fantasy. She knew if she showed this woman her bruises, the most she could do was call Child Protective Services. Then CPS might call, or worse, come to Minh's house. The CPS officers would see the quartz rocks and the rosebushes and the welcome mat at Minh's front door. Both of Minh's parents had steady, respectable jobs, and they were charming and polite with strangers. Minh could imagine the officers sitting at her dining room table, sipping her mom's tea, and laughing as they said *So sorry for the misunderstanding.*

And then when they left, the beatings would be monstrous, her father's hands hammering down on her skin. Her mother slapping wildly until Minh begged for mercy.

"Tell me, Minh. What is going *on?*" her teacher pleaded, interrupting Minh's thoughts.

Minh looked at the choir teacher, sitting in front of her, so put together and unaware. She meant well, but she knew nothing. And there was no way for Minh to explain, really. Because even deeper than the ache of Minh's bruised skin was the hurt in her heart. She was, and always would be, a child who believed that the monsters she lived with were her parents and that they *had* to be good people. Maybe confusing and scary, but she thought if she could just please and obey them, they would come around and love her instead of abuse her.

She believed this every time her dad raped her or when her mom dropped her off at the brothel. She believed it every time she came home and watched them count up her money with a smile. She believed it as she shook her head and repeated, "Nothing much. Just tired, I swear."

It was the only way she could survive.

> **❝** *I think that my parents showed approval like* Oh you made me feel good because you made me money. *Or* Oh that brings me status. *But the approval that I wanted was just sort of* I love you because of who you are, *which they never showed.* **❞**

~ Minh Dang

Justice Is ...

When Minh graduated from high school, her parents agreed to let her go to the University of California, Berkeley as long as she continued to work for them. San Jose was just a short car trip away, so they arranged "tricks" for her and continued to get her back to campus on time when her night routine was over. Again, Minh aced her classes and impressed all her teachers. Nobody in the dorms knew where she went at night or on weekends, and it seemed like she could go on like this indefinitely without anyone noticing.

But being away from home was confusing. Minh saw all of her new college friends going out to parties or pulling all-nighters just to talk about the boy they'd met the night before. She actually went out and *played* for the first time. She took day trips to San Francisco and ran around Pier 39. She ate sourdough bread and listened to music she'd never heard. Even the freedom to go to the campus library seemed magical to Minh.

When her parents ferried her back and forth to the brothel at night, she stared out the car window, trying to figure out why only *her* life had to be locked up in this other world of pain. She thought for the first time that maybe there was a way out.

There was also a part of Minh that was getting louder. During her freshman year she started going to social action meetings on campus. She found out that Asian American immigrants were being deported without really being given a chance to defend themselves. She went to her first public protest and was blown away. She couldn't believe that a group of total strangers from the community had rallied to support an immigrant boy who was going to be deported for no reason. Everyone marched and chanted to show their love and support for someone they didn't even know.

It was so empowering and moving. So far from what she'd grown up seeing.

Huh? People care about strangers? My whole family doesn't care about each other! Minh thought.

She signed up for more meetings and marched in more rallies. The energy of everyone shouting and cheering was addictive. She even organized a demonstration to protest the admissions policies at UC Berkeley and saw how her voice could lead to concrete change. Part of her wondered if maybe, somehow, some way, people could ever hear her story and march for her life to change, too.

One of the organizations Minh joined was called REACH!. It was all about community building and organizing for social justice. Minh loved the other people in this group. Everyone was so passionate about speaking out for their beliefs.

But one day at a meeting, the students were told to hold off on starting any new projects. The faculty was getting concerned that a lot of people from REACH! were skipping class and getting bad grades because they were spending too much time at rallies. Of course for Minh, this wasn't an issue. She was used to going to school, doing afternoon activities, poring over her books, and then going to the brothel most nights. She'd figured out how to exist on little to no sleep.

Still, that meeting stuck with her. She felt like a hypocrite. Here she was supporting everyone else while her parents were still selling her at night. She wasn't sleeping or practicing what she preached at all.

If she really was going to speak out for freedom, didn't it *have* to start with her?

Minh left that meeting, went back to her room, and opened her books. She was looking for some sign, some answer. She found a quote from the activist and philosopher Dr. Cornel West: "Justice is what love looks like in public."

She closed her eyes and imagined Dr. West saying it directly to her. She imagined herself finding some kind of justice, feeling worthy of love.

FICTION: ▰▰▰▰▰▰▰▰▰▰▰▰▰▰▰▰▰▰▰▰

True slaves are chained by shackles.

FACT: ▰▰▰▰▰▰▰▰▰▰▰▰▰▰▰▰▰▰▰▰

A slave is anyone who is treated like someone else's property and/or forced to do work. You don't need chains to be bound. In fact, psychological chains are often harder to break.

Who's the Adult Here?

Minh was motivated and miserable at the same time. She was living two crazy different lives: one where she learned about new philosophies and the power of individual activism, the other where she was being paid or beaten to fulfill someone else's sexual fantasy. She was exhausted from hiding her life at school from her parents and her nights in the brothel from her friends. She continued to meet incredible teachers who inspired her and continued to organize committees for social action with other students. She also started writing poetry, weaving in the images that plagued her. But she didn't know what to do with all of her notebooks and all of the things she wanted to scream to the world.

Minh knew she couldn't live this way anymore. One day during her junior year, she admitted to a therapist on campus that she felt suicidal.

The therapist seemed trustworthy and calm, at least in the beginning. She convinced Minh to withdraw from some of her extracurricular activities and just focus on classes and therapy. Minh still never told her about where she went at night or exactly why it was "complicated" between her and her parents. When she continued to show up at appointments weeping and depressed, the therapist suggested that Minh should go on medication. Minh felt hot with anger when she heard this. She wasn't the one who needed to be medicated. Her sick parents were the ones who needed help. Why couldn't anybody see that Minh was the sane one? She walked out of the therapist's office and swore never to go back again.

Minh felt dizzy and scared, like she was edging her way toward a huge cliff. She could see more open space ahead of her. But it was still such a steep drop, such a huge leap of faith that she could have any life outside of what she'd always known. She'd never had a childhood where anyone had protected her, and she longed for a mother or father or any trustworthy adult to tell her she could make it on her own.

So, Minh kept inching forward. She started lying to her parents. It was never a conscious decision. She told them she would arrange her own tricks and send them the money. The first time she lied, Minh really thought she might be struck by a bolt of lightning. She had been not only an obedient daughter, but also a *slave* to her parents for so many years. Her mom had convinced her that she could always tell if Minh was even thinking about lying.

Minh didn't know how she could possibly get away with it. She dialed her parents' number and sucked in a huge breath.

"The traveling to and from San Jose is really affecting my studies," she explained carefully. She knew her parents were complex people. They wanted to own her, but they also really valued education and wanted her to graduate from college. "I'll get some dates out here and send you the money," Minh said, her voice steady and low. "I promise," she added for good measure.

There was a long pause while Minh clenched her fists and waited for her mom to scream. Instead, she heard a sigh, and then a slow, "Oh … kay."

Minh couldn't believe it worked. It was so simple and revolutionary at the same time. She was convincing her parents and herself at that very moment that she couldn't go on living this way—that she deserved to be free. She rarely arranged any dates or tricks, of course. She saw her parents less and less. When her mom called to ask about the money, Minh just said, "I need it for books."

She imagined herself ripping off shackles, unleashing herself. Minh felt delirious and terrified all at once. And she had no idea what would happen next.

66

Freedom is a state of existence and a process.
Freedom is physical, emotional, and spiritual...
Freedom is quiet.
Freedom is loud.
Freedom is grief—grief that is so deep that it
brings relief, joy, and a sense of the world
expanding.

99

~ Minh Dang

A Matter of Life and Death

One day Minh got a call from her parents. They told
her that her dad was diagnosed with liver cancer. The
doctors did not give him long to live. Minh listened to
her dad talking quietly into the phone. He sounded so
helpless and small.

This was the same man who had beaten and
sexually abused her regularly for the past seventeen
years. The same man who forced her to give up her
body to total strangers and allowed her to be used

and abused by anyone with cash to spare. This was the same man who helped create her and who also destroyed her.

Minh listened to his shaky voice and she knew two things: He was about to die, and she couldn't wait.

She didn't want him to die before she was able to stand up to him. She knew she had to confront him and tell him how much she hated him and how much he had wronged her. She just had no idea *how*.

As Minh's dad got weaker, her mom got more confused and erratic. She called Minh constantly, insisting she was going to divorce Minh's dad and Minh would have to take care of him from now on. At one point, her mom did leave their home in San Jose, but she gave Minh's dad the address of where she was going, and he went and brought her back.

Minh could barely breathe. Everything in her screamed to drop out of school and run away. She tried to tell her mom and dad that what they did to her was cruel and unacceptable. They told her she was making it all up and they had never mistreated her. It was as if they were crawling into her brain and trying to reconfigure her memories. Minh wasn't going back to San Jose anymore and she wasn't arranging tricks, but she felt like she was still under their control. The more she thought about it, the more it became clear to Minh that her parents were never going to change.

Her mother had been throwing Minh into a cage with her poisonous, ravenous father for her whole life. If and when he died, Minh knew she would still be under her mother's reign unless she did something definitive and final.

Minh started the process of changing everything—her phone number, her e-mail, her street address. She opened her own bank account and bought running sneakers so she could sprint through the hills of Berkeley until she felt breathless. Even though she knew this was the only way to climb out, it was incredibly painful for Minh. She felt like she was pulling out the stitches that held her together. Her parents had made her who she was, and she had no idea who she would be once she was emancipated.

Then, on April 14, 2006, Minh sat down at her desk and wrote each of her parents a long e-mail.

She told them that what they had done to her was brutal and inhumane. Instead of parents, they were her torturers. She was done waiting for them to evolve into decent, loving human beings. She was now independent. She told them she was graduating from Berkeley and would never give them a forwarding address. If they tried to track her down ever again, she would contact the police.

She pressed *send* and felt her whole being quake. Her body, her mind, her heart, and her soul were completely hers for the first time. She felt like a newborn baby—naked, vulnerable, and seeing the world for the first time.

The next day, Minh opened her journal and wrote another note. This time to herself.

April 15, 2006 ... FREEDOM DAY.

> 66
I would say I didn't really have a favorite color until I was free.

~ Minh Dang

Rock Party

There were no Fourth of July-style firecrackers or parades when Minh declared her independence. It was actually one of the scariest moments of her life. After all, she'd been enslaved for most of her life. Minh now knew who she *wasn't*—a slave, a sex worker, a victim. But she still had to figure out who she *was*.

She started at the beginning. She'd never had a chance just to be a kid. She'd missed out on making mud pies and throwing temper tantrums. Not once had she hung out at the mall with friends or giggled over some new boy in class. She didn't know what her favorite song was or how to lie peacefully in her bed at night and close her eyes so she could dream.

Sleep was a huge challenge for Minh. For her whole life, she was used to catching just a few winks of sleep either on the way to or from the brothel. Her bedroom at home was a torture chamber. She longed for memories of someone tucking her in and whispering *sleep tight.* So, one of the first steps in her recovery was learning how to turn off her light and trust that it was safe to sink her head into the pillow.

Easier said than done.

The nightmares were fierce and breathtaking. She often lay there just waiting for the sun to rise so she could go out for a jog.

At the same time, Minh was incredibly hopeful. She made sure she went to therapy regularly, and she joined a bunch of support groups for survivors of trafficking and abuse. Slowly, she began to tell her story. There were so many details she'd blocked out or had sworn never to name. Sometimes it felt impossible to figure out what, who, when, and, of course, *why* she was abused and sold. A fellow survivor gave Minh a big three-ring binder and told her to label the tabs in chronological order. On each page she wrote down whatever memories she could dig up. A huge part of recovery, she learned, was getting clear on what had happened and when. This way she could stop keeping it all a secret, really own how horrific it was, and, hopefully, move forward into her new reality.

It was excruciating to report to that binder all the images that she just wanted to obliterate. Many times, she wanted to drop out of therapy and shut the door to the whole world. She was starting to see that she didn't deserve what was done to her. Yet, she could never take back her past, and that made her so upset that it rattled her insides.

So Minh continued to show up to therapy and share her writing. When she did, she felt an incredible release. She screamed and sobbed about her scars, on her skin and in her thoughts. She raged about the fact that she never had a true mommy or daddy. One day in group therapy, Minh realized she didn't know what her favorite color was. "When you're a slave, you don't get to have anything!" she yelled. There were lots of sympathetic nods and tears. Everyone there knew what it was like to start from the beginning.

Minh also went on a lot of survivor retreats where she pitched tents in the wilderness and climbed mountain peaks. She'd always loved the outdoors, and there was no better feeling to her than hiking until her cheeks were flushed and gulping in the sharp, clean air. There was one secret that kept clogging up her brain on these retreats, though. Every time she went backpacking along a new trail, she felt the urge to collect rocks. She saw their layers of sediment, the jagged edges and glittering minerals, and she just wanted to tuck a few in her pocket.

Then she'd hear an angry voice scolding her. *What the *#$@ are these doing here?* Minh walked faster, trying to march over the voice, but it continued. *You're worthless! You're dirty!* She stamped her feet. *You made your father choose you over me!*

Minh told her survivor friends about her long gone, but not forgotten, rock collection. Their response? A rock party! Everyone invited was told to find a rock that Minh would love. Minh was stunned that people could hear her and care about her this much. One friend told her, "You can collect rocks now if you want and it's not because you can't talk to people because clearly you have plenty of people to talk to. But I hope you talk to them because that was a beautiful survival tool and also just a beautiful thing you did—seeing the beauty in those rocks."

Minh's rock collection grew. She spent more and more time outdoors—hiking, joining a soccer league, and getting serious about running. She loved the feel of her pulse pounding in her ears and the flood of adrenaline that filled her whole body. She finally felt alive. She finally started appreciating her body—her muscles and bones, her stamina and grace.

She forced herself to look all around, to find new colors, new rocks, new skies that she'd never seen before she was free. It was as if all the elements were speaking to her—whispering secrets on how to live in this brand-new world. Even the clouds could teach her something.

Running with the Rain

I took a moment to feel the rain on my body and I felt a full-body sigh pass through me.

This is what life is about: feeling in my body and being in the present moment.

I thought to myself, 'Well, I guess you're running in the rain today.'

And then, from somewhere else inside of myself, I said, 'No. Run WITH the rain.'

I wasn't exactly sure what I meant by this until I got home and Googled 'Why does it rain?'

It rains because water from oceans and rivers evaporates when it's warm, and then when it's cold, water condenses, forms clouds, and eventually gravity pulls droplets of water down and we have rain.

So…why does it rain? Because water does what it's meant to do.

And then it clicked for me…

Run WITH the rain. Do what you are meant to do. Do what nature intended. For me, and I believe for each of us, nature intended that we

LIVE,
LOVE,
and BE FREE

~ Minh Dang

> **"**
> *My life is gonna be about changing the world.*
> **"**
>
> ~ Minh Dang

I Have Something to Say

Minh sprinted through the streets of Berkeley, rain or shine. Even when she came back from a run drenched and muddy, she felt triumphant and so grateful for the legs that had carried her here.

One of the things Minh kept coming back to was how college had helped transform her life. She felt empowered studying social movements and seeing how individuals could make real change in society. It also helped that she had amazing professors who appreciated her work and really listened to her ideas.

By the time Minh graduated and emancipated from her parents, she knew she wanted to continue her education. She felt a strong connection between education and political action, and she loved how she was being valued at school for her mind, her heart, and her intentions, not her body.

Minh applied for a student loan to pursue a master's degree in social work at Berkeley. Before she even started the graduate program, Minh got a job as an advisor to undergrads. One day, a student showed up at her office and asked Minh casually, "Do you know anybody who maybe knows something about human trafficking?"

Minh took in a deep breath before answering, "Yeah, I do."

It was one thing to talk about her experiences in therapy or support group. Telling someone outside of those safe walls felt like walking a tightrope—on stilts. At the same time, something in the student's face looked so honest and kind, and Minh knew that part of her healing involved speaking out.

"I was trafficked, actually," Minh heard herself say. The student's eyes grew wide and watery. The room was as quiet and still as snow. It took a few minutes for both of them to catch their breath. Then the student thanked Minh over and over again for her honesty and bravery. She asked if Minh would please speak at a kickoff symposium for her new anti-trafficking campaign.

Minh politely declined. She wanted to help this young woman and she obviously believed in the cause, but everything was too new and raw for any sort of public "outing." She needed to make sure that anybody who heard her would listen to her as a human being, not as some freak of nature. Minh was still filled with so much fear and shame about her past, as if she had somehow *asked* to be a slave.

The student looked disappointed but said she understood. Minh promised to come and support her, but silently.

The night of the symposium, Minh staked out a spot in the middle of the room. It was one of the medium-sized lecture halls on campus, but not many seats were empty, which was more than fine for Minh. She just wanted to be as close to an exit sign as possible. She didn't think she'd make it through listening to all the presenters, and she planned to slip out whenever it got to be too overwhelming for her.

What Minh didn't plan on was the Oakland Police.

These were the same officers from the neighborhood where she grew up. They had walked by the rosebushes and quartz rocks and the crime scene that was her life. But, she'd never reported her parents because of the guilt, dread, and shame that weighed her down.

So, when an Oakland Police officer stood up at the podium and talked about johns and pimps like they were mustachioed "bad guys" in a cartoon, and all the young victims as scraggly runaways, Minh knew she had to shout her truth.

She cleared her throat and said, "Actually I'm a survivor of human trafficking, and we need to be thinking about why the girls are on the street in the first place. What homes are they coming from? My parents were my perpetrators, and actually I don't know the statistics, but I know a lot of survivors just in my life who were trafficked by their own parents. So it's not just about like johns and stranger pimps."

When she was done talking, Minh felt like her whole body was on fire. She heard cheers and applause, but she didn't dare look around to see people's faces. She wished there were some sort of trap door or eject button so she could launch herself into outer space.

The rest of the symposium was blurry for Minh. There were closing remarks and more clapping. She wanted to leave but also felt glued to the floor, trying to slow her breath down. Minh was just getting out the door when a producer from MSNBC came up to her and told her she was phenomenal. It wasn't just because her story was amazing; it was *how* she told her story that was amazing. Then she asked Minh if she would speak on camera about her childhood for a documentary.

Minh thanked the producer and said no, she wasn't ready for that. At least, not yet.

Minh started her graduate program, burying herself in books again, only this time it wasn't to escape her life; it was to create a new one. She learned all the essential skills to become a trained therapist and social worker, like good interviewing techniques, how to be truly present with a person, how to work with different populations, how to diagnose mental and emotional disorders, and how to create an effective treatment plan.

The workload was hard and emotionally intense. Minh decided early on that she was most excited about working with *transition age youth,* who are people between the ages of eighteen and twenty-five. That's how old she was when she freed herself. That's when children legally become adults and get so many new responsibilities like voting, drinking, figuring out health insurance, and independence. And Minh was surprised to learn in her science classes that it's also the age when human brains fully develop.

When her professor said this, Minh couldn't believe it. She jotted it down in her notes to be polite, but it felt impossible. Then she went back to her apartment, went online, and Googled it. Every medical journal said the same thing. Minh stared at her computer screen and felt a smile inch across her lips. She now had scientific proof that she'd been a victim and not a perpetrator. All the voices of fear and shame that told her she "chose" to stay and be abused or that she "asked for it" had to listen up.

Even though her classmates in school had celebrated sweet sixteens, bar mitzvahs, and driver's licenses; even though Minh had been treated like an adult (sexually) since she was three, the truth was that human beings weren't truly mature until much later. Learning this made Minh feel so relieved and reenergized. For the first time she saw not only how she could start over, but also how she could help other people her age discover themselves, too.

66 ▓▓▓▓▓▓▓▓▓▓▓▓▓▓▓▓

And so, I've super transformed my wardrobe because it was a lot about thinking my body, or my dress, caused what happened. And that's a lot more palatable than to just think, no, actually somebody else just wants to hurt me.

▓▓▓▓▓▓▓▓ **99**

~ Minh Dang

Reclaiming Beauty

Minh's favorite thing to wear in 1990: a soccer uniform, shin guards, and pigtails.

Why? The soccer field was the one place where Minh could be a kid. She could get muddy and sweaty, kick fiercely, and run full speed ahead. When she had her eye on the soccer ball, there was no fear or confusion holding her back. Minh was focused and powerful, and she knew she only had one thing to do—*play.*

Minh's favorite thing to wear in 2005: baggy jeans, running shoes, and a dark hoodie (preferably two sizes too big so she could pull the hood over her eyes). This was what Minh wore almost every day through college. Even though she was reading, writing, and even organizing events about self-determination and social activism, Minh felt like she had to look as unnoticeable as possible. She wanted people to value her thoughts, not scope out her figure. She honestly didn't know how her head and the rest of her body could one day fit together.

Minh's favorite thing to wear in 2014: a coral-striped, strapless sundress, glittery hoop earrings, and a touch of mascara.

Who? Yes, Minh. The first time she tried on this outfit and looked in the mirror, she heard herself gasp. She felt *hot*.

Then she felt incredibly ashamed.

What if people thought she was *trying* to look hot? Would she be solicited on campus? Was she asking to be used and abused all along?

She pulled out the earrings and shoved the dress into her backpack, put her hoodie-jeans outfit on, and marched back to group therapy.

"I don't want to fear my own reflection anymore!" she announced. "What happened to me has nothing to do with how I dress, right? It was not my fault!"

Her fellow survivors knew this anger and self-consciousness too well. It was hard for any of them to look in the mirror and enjoy the curve of their hips, or even the color of their eyes. "Not your fault," they echoed. "Put that dress back on and enjoy what it feels like to be sexy!"

Minh started slowly substituting khaki skirts for her jeans. Then she switched out the dark hoodie with a teal half-sweater when she was feeling a little stronger. It was easier if she stepped back from her mirror and pretended she was dressing a mannequin. Some days, the rush of memories was too intense—her parents forcing her to wear see-through lingerie as she greeted another stranger at the brothel; the smell of her stockings as she peeled them off in the car.

Again, being in school helped a lot. On a practical level, Minh's graduate program included advising students and presenting papers. She couldn't exactly speak in front of classes and professors in baggy jeans and expect them to take her seriously. Also, she was studying the very ideas she was struggling with, like how slavery and exploitation were passed down through the generations. She *knew* in her heart that there was no problem in dressing sexy. The problem was in having it exploited.

Minh was very attractive with dark, intense eyes, smooth olive skin, and a small but muscular frame.

Her smile was thoughtful and made everyone around her feel special. The more she spoke about reclaiming beauty, the more she believed in it. The more she believed in it, the more she smiled.

One day she found herself smiling next to a guy at a friend's party. Minh was smiling a lot. Laughing and blushing, too. The guy was definitely into her as well, cracking her up with jokes and telling her about his family. Minh knew she was attracted to people who appreciated family.

They exchanged numbers and set up a time to go jogging together.

After that, there was a trip to Minh's favorite café. Then a day at an art fair, followed by the movies. And then an awkward pause as they said good-bye. *Was this feeling okay?* Minh wondered. To be attracted to someone and want to spend more time with him, even hold him? To trust someone this much?

When Minh had her first real kiss—unforced and unexpected—it was both terrifying and exhilarating. She felt attracted to this guy physically and intellectually, which she'd never thought possible before. At the same time, she felt incredibly triggered by having anyone touch her sensually. She knew if this relationship were going to go anywhere, she'd one day have to tell him about her past and share her vision for the future.

Ssssh! she begged her brain to stop racing ahead or behind.

She only wanted to drift into this new bubbly space of sly smiles and nervous hiccups. This beautiful moment called the present.

66

'Survivor' is not a title. It's not what defines a person. Survivors have interests and skills, favorite colors and pet peeves, hopes and dreams, and sorrows and regrets. Just like all human beings, survivors are complex, multifaceted people.

99

~ Minh Dang

Are You *the* Minh Dang?

In 2010, Minh was in a documentary called "Sex Slaves in America." (That MSNBC producer from the Oakland Police symposium never gave up on her.)

After that, Minh's phone was ringing off the hook with people asking her to come tell her story at schools, shelters, conferences, and teacher trainings. Minh wasn't into it at first. She had no intention of making her life so public, and she didn't know how to fit it in with her school life. Her mentors told her she had a real gift for speaking, and the fact that she was on national television meant she could really get people focused on the anti-trafficking movement. Minh realized she had an opportunity to do some powerful political organizing.

The "red carpet" for sex-trafficking survivors was a little different than for movie stars. Minh became a celebrity in the social justice world pretty quickly. She started speaking at human rights conferences, and at survivor coalition and advocacy group meetings, all over the globe. In just a few years, she went from standing in the back of the lecture hall at Berkeley to being a headliner at meetings on Capitol Hill.

Of course, Minh often said she'd rather be famous because she invented the iPhone or discovered a new planet. Still, it was exciting to know she was making such an impact on people's lives, especially when total strangers came up to her after one of her talks and said she was the first one to truly understand. She saw tears of appreciation and relief. People swore she was the one who motivated them to break free, too, or to confront their abusers. The invitations to speak kept coming in.

Minh decided she didn't want just to talk about what had happened to her. She'd rather fight for new policies and laws that would make sure this kind of crime never happened again. She talked about the importance of better mental health services and training for new parents. She wanted people who'd suffered trauma to be covered under mental health insurance. She said college should be free and the minimum wage had to be raised. Again, audiences were amazed at her powerful voice and the way she not only survived, but also made her life all about giving when so much had been taken from her. In 2013, Minh was asked to visit the White House to receive an award as a Champion of Change and speak there about her dedication to end human trafficking.

Flying from a gig in London to one in Washington, D.C., and stopping off in Malibu on the way home wasn't half bad. Minh was amazed at how quickly her world opened up and how many people were interested in her story. At one conference, she overheard a woman say breathlessly, "What? You got to talk to *the* Minh Dang?"

Minh was touched, but she also started freaking out a little bit. The responsibility of being a survivor spokeswoman was a lot to carry on her shoulders. After each presentation, she had people lining up to tell her their tragic stories, asking for advice, or calling her a superhero.

The superhero part is what bothered Minh the most. She didn't want people to separate her from the rest of humanity anymore. She felt so isolated and misunderstood when people told her they could never be as brave as she was. She felt like a caged animal at the zoo, or an alien, living and thinking on a different plane, separated from all humanity.

So, when Minh wasn't speaking, she was writing. She wrote about reconnecting with her humanity and the humanity of others. She didn't want to feel like an alien anymore. She wrote: *Survivors are NO DIFFERENT than you are. You are no different than I am. If you were born to my parents and put in the exact same situation, you would be writing this right now. Find a way to relate with survivors. You do not need to have gone through what they went through to imagine what they might experience.*

When Minh wasn't writing in her journals, she was blogging for Don't Sell Bodies, an anti-trafficking organization that offers information and gets celebrities and activists from all over the world to rally together. Jada Pinkett Smith (a very talented actress, activist, and star of the *Madagascar* movies) founded the organization. She asked Minh to come on board as executive director and write on the DSB website about what it felt like to break free and live a new life.

Minh's writing was raw and honest. Even when she wrote about what it felt like to be free, she refused to decorate her new world with rainbows or unicorns.

She wrote the real stuff—what it felt like to mourn parents who were never there for her. How it stung to trust and fall in love for the first time, only to have her heart broken. She wrote about how she was *not* a superhero, about how she never drank a courage pill or wished upon some secret star.

She was human, struggling to live her life humanely, gratefully every day.

> *I have had to learn (or re-learn) that I am human, I was always human, and that the people out there, you, as well as those who hurt me, are also human.*

> 〞
>
> ~ Minh Dang

The Heart That Feels Pain

Minh woke up at 5:30 A.M. The moon was the only light making leaf shadows on her wall. She lay still and waited for some of the birds to wake up, too. She heard a branch creak on the big oak tree in her garden. Down the road, there was a car door opening and shutting.

These early morning hours were the hardest for Minh. She still had trouble sleeping for more than a few hours at a time. Her body had been conditioned for so long to stay alert and on guard when night came. She counted anything past 5:00 A.M. as morning and made lists of things to do to help motivate herself for the day. Her morning could include meditating or journaling or calling a friend. She also had a gratitude jar that she was slowly filling with slips of paper, naming everything and everyone she loved.

On this particular morning, Minh decided to first turn on her "Morning Love" playlist. This was something she added to every time she found a song that helped her feel loved or inspired. Minh pulled back the covers and climbed down the small ladder from her loft bed. The wooden floor felt cool as she padded over to her laptop on the desk and cued up her music.

The first song—her favorite—was Ingrid Michaelson's "Everybody."

Happy is the heart that still feels pain, sang Ingrid. Minh started her teakettle and did a few stretches on the small patch of linoleum near her stove. She looked around her, trying to take it all in.

She still couldn't believe this place was hers. Every inch of it. It was a small cottage in Berkeley, really one large room, painted the color of melting butter and sunshine. Her desk and books were built into one wall and the rest of the room was open windows. There was a wood-burning stove in the corner and the loft hovering just under the ceiling. Outside Minh's door was a small, lush garden. It was a far cry from the white quartz rocks and rosebushes back in San Jose. Minh's backyard was sprawling and wildflowers yawned open, up and down the path. She had a punching bag hung from a tree where she often sparred and cross-jabbed her way out of her darkest spells of anger.

This was Minh's first home of her own. She moved here in 2013. It was everything she wanted: light, open, close to hiking trails and great restaurants. Yet, she found it incredibly lonely sometimes. She was on the road a lot for her speaking engagements. She also was consulting for counselor trainings and finishing her dissertation for school.

"How will you love yourself today?" read the sign Minh had posted to her bathroom mirror. That was a good question. Minh knew she had a lot of writing to do on her thesis. She was supposed to be giving a new talk in three days in New York. She could maybe stop at the farmer's market for flowers or squeeze in a massage. But really, all she could think about was the PTA.

This was the dream that had awoken her at 5:30. This was the dream she kept having, and she wanted so badly to make true. In it, Minh was a mom of two little children. Their faces were unclear but their eyes were big and dark, just like hers. She saw their crayon pictures hanging in the school hallway and said proudly, "Those are my kids'." Then she walked into a classroom and spoke to the PTA about the upcoming book drive and invited everyone over to her house for a game night with popcorn. As she drove home from the meeting, she knew every tree and every lamppost. It was familiar and safe. Her front door was unlocked. When she walked in she could smell the frittata she had made that morning for her family.

Minh had this PTA dream a lot. And whenever she awoke, she didn't know whether to laugh or cry. She knew she had to have a life where she could speak out about human justice and defending freedom. But what if her form of social activism was raising two happy children and making a home filled with her children's drawings and the smell of freshly popped popcorn?

There were still a lot of blanks to fill in. She was feeling giddy about a new boy she was seeing. *Was he ready to have kids?* she wondered. Was she? And what about her writing and speaking career? She loved all her work consulting and training, and she had even started running self-empowerment retreats. She loved hearing people share their hopes, dreams, and hungers. She felt purposeful and passionate talking to young adults about who she once was, and how she broke free.

The teakettle whistled. Minh poured the hot water into her favorite mug and let the tea steep. She stood by her open door, a soft fog coloring the morning light purple.

"Lots of work, but maybe meet at the farmer's market later?" Minh texted the boy she'd been seeing. She didn't want to be too eager, but she was a firm believer in making herself open to possibilities. She didn't wait for his answer.

Instead, she laced up her sneakers, pulled on a sweatshirt and shorts, and took a few sips of her tea before heading out for a run.

Her feet were sure. Her stride was long and fast. She passed a clump of cafés, a yoga studio, a playground. She loved her new route, its bends and twists. She tried to memorize the names of the streets even though they looked blurry. She looped around the playground again. This time she stopped. It took her a moment to recognize what was making her blink.

It was the rain. It was the sky opening up and letting go. It was everything she wanted to learn and become.

This is what life is about: feeling in my body and being in the present moment. I thought to myself, "Well, I guess you're running in the rain today." And then, from somewhere else inside of myself, I said, "No. Run WITH the rain."

Maria Suarez

Everyone Is Family

Maria grew up in a small village in Mexico called Timbuscatio, Michoacan. There were only about 500 or so people in Timbuscatio, and most of them were related to one another. Maria was eleventh out of fourteen children in her family. When her brothers and sisters were too busy to play with her, she could always knock on a door nearby and find a cousin ready to play hide and seek in the cornfields. Even the people she wasn't related to knew and loved her as if they were family, too.

Maria's father was a farmer. He worked long days, up before dawn planting corn, *calavasa*, pumpkin, sugarcane, cucumber, tomatoes, corn, and guava. His hands were thick and stained from pulling through the earth. His rectangular face was always flushed from the sun. Maria's mom was always working, too. She took care of the fourteen children and the house, not to mention feeding their chickens, turkeys, pigs, cows, and goats. The only time Maria saw her sit still was in church on Sundays. Maria's mom sang all the psalms and listened to the priest with her eyes half-shut, a smile taking up the rest of her face. Maria loved watching her mom so serene and happy. Maria sat next to her in the pews, a matching smile taking up her face, too.

When Maria was fifteen years old, her father announced that he needed to go to Los Angeles to get an American residential card.

Why can't we live here forever? Maria wondered.

Her parents would never tell her, but it was getting harder and harder to feed the family. Her father didn't want to leave Timbuscatio either, but his fields were looking thin and dry. He promised he would be back in a few weeks; he just needed to see if it was possible to get some steady income in the States.

Maria begged her dad to bring her on the trip. She promised to stay out of trouble and bring her schoolbooks so she didn't miss any lessons while she was away. He agreed. When they got to California, Maria and her dad stayed with an older sister living and working in Sierra Madre. Maria decided that if she really wanted to help the family out, she should look for work, too. It was harder than she expected, though. She didn't speak any English, and she didn't know exactly what work she could offer.

A kind-looking woman walked up to Maria on the street one day and asked her—in Spanish!—if she was looking for a job. Maria was so grateful to hear her native language and immediately said, "Si." The woman was searching for a maid to help out in an old couple's home. Maria was thrilled and tried not to laugh out loud while she said, again, "Si! Si!" She was so excited, she even forgot to ask how much the job paid.

They set a time for the woman to pick up Maria and take her to the couple's house. The woman said Maria should keep it a surprise and not tell her family.

Maria didn't know why it had to be a secret, but she was too excited to ask. She was already dreaming about coming back to the farm with a wallet full of hard-earned cash. Maybe she would buy her mom a new dress, or her dad a hat to protect his eyes from the sun …

FICTION:

Witches wear black hats, ride broomsticks, and have warts.

FACT:

Brujo is Spanish for male witch. A *brujo* can look like everyone else, but many cultures, especially Mexican, believe *brujos* can cast magical spells to either help or curse people.

A Tomorrow That Never Comes

Maria knew something was not right. The trip to the old couple's house was taking much too long. She stared out the woman's car window and felt like the roads were all twisting into oblivion. Maria didn't know why she'd left without telling her sister where she was going. The surprise of a new job wasn't feeling exciting anymore. The longer Maria sat in that car, the more she felt like she was riding away from everyone she knew, straight off the map into the unknown.

Maria and the woman drove almost the whole way in silence. Whenever Maria asked where they were, the woman told her it was close and not to worry. They pulled into a driveway in front of a small house. The town they were in now was called Azusa, California. Long, elegant palm trees were overhead and a Masonic temple was next door. Maria felt a little better after she saw a sign for the neighborhood doctor's office that was nearby. Maybe she had been worried about nothing all along. This place looked friendly enough, at least from the outside.

The old man who answered the door gave her a warm hello. Maria guessed him to be about sixty-five or seventy. He closed the door quickly and led her into the living room, where he told her to sit on the couch. Then he and the woman disappeared into the kitchen and talked in low mumbles.

Maria didn't know what they were saying. She just knew she wanted to get out of there. It didn't look like the place needed a maid. There was barely any furniture, and if there was dust it was too dark to tell. There was no sunlight—the shades were drawn and the air was so stuffy and thick. The only thing Maria could hear was herself panting.

When the old man came back into the room, he told her she was hired.

Maria thanked him and said she should probably get home and check with her family first.

The old man shook his head no. He wanted Maria to start working today, and he promised he'd take her home tomorrow. He insisted that his wife was due home soon and would be so happy to meet Maria.

Maria didn't like his plan, but the woman who drove her said she couldn't drive her back anyway.

"You can even call your sister if you want," the old man said with a smile. He walked her to the phone in the kitchen. Before Maria could dial, he had to unlock the receiver. Maria had never seen a lock on a phone.

Maria's sister was not happy with the situation. She said Maria needed to come home immediately. Maria tried to explain that the man was old and that they were waiting for his wife to return.

"Where are you, exactly?" Maria's sister demanded.

Maria had no idea where she was. She just kept repeating that she'd be home tomorrow. She wished there were a way to tell her sister how she was really feeling, but with the old man standing inches away from her, she couldn't find the words.

After she hung up the phone, the woman who'd driven her left. Maria heard the front door slam shut. The old man locked it with a bolt. When he turned around to face Maria again, his smile got even bigger. And creepier.

He offered to show Maria around the house. In the room where she would sleep, Maria saw an altar with a picture of Jesus Christ in the middle. There was also a line of little bottles filled with dirt and dolls with pins stuck all over their bodies. That first night, Maria pulled the blanket over her face so she couldn't see the dolls. She prayed for tomorrow to come as fast as possible.

The next day, the old man greeted Maria with a mop and a pile of rags. He said he'd take her home as soon as she was done making the place spotless. She scrubbed every shelf and sill in the house. She mopped and re-mopped the floors. But every time she told the old man she was done, he shook his head no.

The phone was locked. The door was locked. Night came and Maria hid under the covers again.

On the third day, the man told her she could stop cleaning, but he had other things for her to do. Lots of other things. And she wasn't going home any time soon because he'd paid two hundred dollars for her to stay.

"Do you know why?" he asked. He smiled again, as if they were playing some exciting guessing game. Maria shook her head no. She didn't want to know.

"You're mine now," he said. "To cook, to clean, to pleasure me in any way."

Maria shook and shook. She shook so hard, trying to wipe away this moment from her brain and erase it from being possible. The man was still talking, telling her that if she tried to contact her family, he would kill her or them.

This is not happening. This cannot be real. Maria shook her head faster and faster.

The man explained that he was a *brujo* and everyone in the town knew it. He promised he could read Maria's mind and make her worst nightmares come true. Nobody would stop him, either. Even the priests in the temple next door knew he was a witch who practiced black magic, and they were terrified of him.

Then, just to prove his point, the old man tore off all Maria's clothes. Maria shrieked and tried to grab them back. As she reached for them, he punched Maria in the face, and he kept punching until everything went dark.

When she came to, she was lying on the ground with her clothes next to her. At this point she was painfully aware of two things: One, that she had been raped, and two, that no matter how much she screamed or cried, there was nobody there to help her.

> *Sometimes when I think about it and I wonder, it was because of my brown skin? It was because we're not on the high class? It was because I didn't speak any English? You know what I mean? How can they assume I was okay?*
>
> ~ Maria Suarez

Doing What She's Told

Whether he was a witch or not, the old man definitely had a hold on Maria. He told her every day how he would kill her family if she tried to escape. He was very convincing, too. He barely moved his face when he spoke, except to give her that same creepy smile.

It was as if the whole town was under his spell. Maria saw people through the curtains, walking in and out of the doctor's office and the temple. But they all seemed to walk *around* the old man's house, being careful not even to touch his lawn with the edge of a shoe. At one point, the old man forced Maria to work in a factory nearby to bring him more money. When Maria tried to hide in the bathroom until everyone left, her boss pulled her out and sent her back to the old man for an even more vicious beating.

Lying on the ground, bruised and weak, Maria started thinking, *Either he's going to kill me or I'm going to die.* And dying didn't sound all that bad anymore.

The old man continued to beat and molest Maria regularly. She was in a constant haze of fear and disbelief. She kept working and doing what she was told because she couldn't see any alternatives.

The only place Maria didn't work was in the small guesthouse in the old man's backyard. He rented it to a young couple, and though Maria never went in she was pretty sure that the old man visited the guesthouse to pursue the wife, too. Maria didn't know if they'd been lured here by the same woman who had promised Maria a job. She just knew they were all caught in this man's grip and there was no way out.

One day, Maria heard shrieks coming from the backyard followed by a loud whacking sound. Maria wanted to pretend she couldn't hear anything, but then she thought of all those neighbors walking by, ignoring her screams, and she knew she couldn't do the same.

The first thing she saw was blood inching through the grass.

Then she saw a plank of wood, soaked a deep red.

She saw the wife's mouth open, screaming, and her husband stroking her hair.

Maria saw it all, but her brain could not process any of it, especially once she looked down and saw her torturer, the old man, splayed out on the ground. His smile was gone. His skull was cracked open and leaking into the earth.

The renter picked up the plank of wood that he'd just used to murder the old man and pushed it toward Maria. She just blinked, her eyes still not believing this could be true. He instructed her to bury it under the house. She felt like a zombie, her body separated from her brain. She followed the renter's orders, digging through the dirt and burying the bloody plank next to the house. She had no idea what else to do. She was so used to following angry orders and commands.

Then the police were there. Maria's sister was there, too. Maria didn't know how or when they came. She was just wandering around the backyard, in a fog of terror. The renter and his wife were sent away.

Maria's sister was still living with her husband and daughter in Sierra Madre. She drove Maria back to her house and rocked Maria in her arms, promising her she was safe now.

But Maria couldn't hear her. She couldn't eat or sleep or even find the words, *I love you, too.* Maria was caught in a loop of nightmares. All she could see was the old man on the ground, splattered with blood. Then Maria saw him pulling himself out of the grass and lunging at her with half of his head gone. She sat in her sister's kitchen, quaking and sweating.

This is where the police found her when they came again.

Maria heard the words, "Maria Suarez, you are under arrest."

Then she heard her sister screaming, "No!"

Maria felt the skin on her wrist catch in the handcuffs.

She smelled the warm vinyl of the police car.

But still, all she could see was the old man reaching for her. *Please,* she thought, *somebody get him out of my head.*

> *I know that I am not guilty. I have not done anything wrong. I just didn't know how to defend myself.*
>
> ~ Maria Suarez

The Sentence

Maria was assigned a lawyer to defend her in court. She didn't understand what he was saying to her. English was still very difficult for her, and his words came at her quickly. She was mashing them all together in her head and couldn't make sense of it all. He also couldn't sit still or look her in the eye. Whenever they met to discuss her case, he paced around the room and checked all the security cameras. He swore he'd get her out of custody soon.

Maria didn't know who or what to believe anymore. She was still having those visions of the old man coming to get her. She couldn't focus, and she got more and more confused every time someone came in to question her.

Her sister came to visit and told her the police were working on her case. Maria nodded silently. Then her sister came back and said the police wouldn't help because there were no reports of abuse from that house. Maria nodded silently again.

"Please tell them what happened!" her sister pleaded.

Maria sat with her lawyer again and tried to describe the house with the altar, the guesthouse, the bloodied plank of wood. Whether she spoke in Spanish or tried in English, her lawyer still didn't get it.

She found out later that her attorney was watching the security cameras instead of looking at her because he had recently been caught selling drugs. He'd also been disbarred and was using someone else's identity to fight her case. But by the time Maria learned all this, it didn't matter. The judge and jury never heard about how she'd been tortured and raped. They just saw the plank of wood and the nervously pacing lawyer and decided she was guilty.

Maria was convicted of conspiracy to murder. She was sentenced to twenty-five years in prison. Another door bolted shut. Maria nodded silently. There was nothing else to say.

> **"**
> *If I'm dreaming about this tunnel with the light far, far away, how am I gonna be able to reach the light if I'm this bitter, dark, helpless person? I need to bring myself back.*
> **"**

~ Maria Suarez

Tunnel Vision

Where are you? I've been calling you over and over! Where are you?

This was Maria's prayer night after night. She knelt on the floor and wept. She honestly felt like God had forgotten about her.

How could you leave me with him?

Maria had been raised Catholic and she knew all the psalms by heart, but she didn't know what she believed in anymore. She felt bitter and abandoned, haunted by this old man who still took over her thoughts. She didn't know if she was hot or cold, hungry or thirsty. Her senses had disappeared. Fear was the only thing she had left.

Maria's mother and sister told her the only way she could be released was to pray. Her mom insisted there was a special saint who could help her, but only if Maria forgave the old man for everything he'd done. Maria felt like forgiving him was impossible after what he'd done to her. She muttered the prayers over and over again, calling on the saint to come save her. She didn't know how it could work, but she was willing to try anything.

Then, Maria's dreams got even darker. Now she saw a narrow tunnel with a dot of light at the far end. It was long and cold and she was struggling to get to that light. She tried walking, running, crawling, scraping her body along the ground. The light kept moving farther away. As she pulled herself toward it, the old man was next to her, ready to pounce.

"Keep praying," her mother implored.

One day, Maria woke up from the tunnel dream choking on huge sobs. She felt like all the tears and pain she'd been storing up and pushing away for the past several years were erupting. She imagined her past as a thick, knotted rope that someone was pulling out of her inch by inch.

She lay on her cot and cried for hours and hours, the bottomless well of hurt and fear coming up and out of her. She couldn't hide from her demons or rush down cold tunnels anymore. She raged and shouted until her throat felt raw and until her brain was blissfully empty.

Then Maria looked around her cell and, for the first time in what felt like forever, she could breathe again.

She glanced up at the ceiling and wondered if God had finally heard her. Or maybe it was the special saint. She didn't need an answer. She just knew in her heart that she had been released.

And now it was time to fight for her freedom.

> ❝
> *In prison, I felt free.*
> ❞
>
> ~ Maria Suarez

Finding Momentum

Maria had only one thing on her mind now. She was determined to go back to school. There were university courses being offered in the state prison and she signed herself up for English first. She wanted to read, write, and speak the language fluently so she could tell her story.

Every time Maria opened one of her textbooks, she saw the letters like stepping stones, leading her out of captivity. She filled up notebook after notebook, memorizing new words and ideas. Her brain felt energized and hungry. She soon signed up for classes in computer science and social work, too, and she started collecting the credits she needed to earn her General Educational Development (GED) degree.

Maria also started working with a doctor in the prison who counseled emotionally troubled prisoners. These were the people who either had emotional difficulties before they got there, or who just couldn't accept that their life was now behind bars. Maria went to some of the doctor's group sessions and held anyone's hand who needed extra compassion as they tried to piece together their thoughts. For the older prisoners, Maria read books or listened to them talk about what they'd been through.

Maria never knew why her fellow inmates had been sentenced, and she didn't feel like she needed to know. Innocent or guilty, young or old, they all had one thing in common: They all were grieving for the lives they'd lost outside of the prison walls. Maria felt that loss, too, and offering a hand or an ear was the most important thing she could think to do. She knew prison would never feel like home, but at least studying and working with that doctor gave her some sort of momentum. It was the most purposeful she'd felt since she was a little girl, carrying in tomatoes off the vine.

Maria's family was in contact with her constantly. Her sister visited her all the time. The two of them tried to keep the visits cheerful, sharing stories and vending machine snacks. Maria wrote letters back and forth with her family in Mexico, too—in Spanish and in English. Even if they couldn't fathom what it was like for her in prison or read this new language she was learning, they could tell she was motivated. They could feel how hard she was working to make each day a new beginning.

They celebrated each and every victory with her. They read her letters out loud and cheered as she described her GED test. They also sadly shared the news that Maria's father was dying, and that he sent his love to her, always.

And, of course, in each letter, call, or visit, Maria and her family counted the days until her next parole review.

FICTION: ▆▆▆▆▆▆▆▆▆▆▆▆▆▆▆▆▆▆▆▆▆

Nobody knows how to stop human trafficking. It's every (wo)man for him or herself.

FACT: ▆▆▆▆▆▆▆▆▆▆▆▆▆▆▆▆▆▆▆▆▆▆

It will definitely be tough to do, but there are incredibly talented and compassionate people working to end human trafficking on a global level. There is now a Global Human Trafficking Hotline Network, where countries all over the globe share information about who has been caught and where, as well as provide protection to victims and survivors wherever they are found.

The Dream Team

It took twenty years before the Board of Prison Terms (BPT) recommended that Maria be released. They called her case "one of the most egregious instances of battered woman syndrome that [the BPT has] ever investigated." The renter from the guesthouse came forward and admitted that Maria had nothing to do with her trafficker's murder.

On December 16, 2003, Governor Arnold Schwarzenegger granted Maria parole.

But instead of walking out of the prison gates and dancing into freedom, two days later she was sent to the U.S. Immigration and Naturalization Services detention center in San Pedro. The law had changed while she was in prison. Anyone who was in the United States with a green card and convicted of a crime had to be deported, even if they were later found innocent. The state prison had taken away her green card as soon as she was arrested. Schwarzenegger refused to give her a pardon and let her stay in America, where her family now lived.

Maria's family was feeling desperate and furious, particularly her niece, Patricia. For almost all of Patricia's life, she'd watched her Aunt Maria studying and counseling in prison. Maria was always the one cheering up Patricia at their visits, telling the young girl to keep hoping and believing. Patricia admired her aunt so much, she wished there were something she could do to challenge this unfair sentence.

Patricia found a lawyer named Jessica Dominguez. Jessica was an immigrant, too, and had just started her own law offices in Los Angeles with a desk she bought at a Salvation Army store and a passion for helping people she thought were mistreated by the American justice system. When Patricia told her

Maria's story, Jessica was horrified and said she would take the case *pro bono* (for free).

Jessica enlisted Charles Song from Los Angeles-based CAST (the Coalition to Abolish Slavery and Trafficking). Jessica and Charles were the first lawyers who listened to Maria's whole story and treated her like a human being instead of a crazed murderer. They added two more lawyer friends to the dream team: Andres Bustamante and Brigit Alvarez. The four of them worked for months and months to get testimony from other people who knew Maria when she was enslaved and even in prison, to show what an honest, hardworking, and forgiving person she was.

Jessica also started organizing rallies and letter-writing campaigns for Maria's cause as an immigrant. Jessica called every elected official she knew. U.S. Representative Hilda Solis, a Democrat from California who would go on to serve as the U.S. Secretary of Labor under President Barack Obama, and Marta Sahagún de Fox, who at the time was the first lady of Mexico, promised they would join the fight to free Maria and keep her in the United States.

Solis helped write a letter to U.S. Secretary of Homeland Security Tom Ridge and Undersecretary for Border and Transportation Security Asa Hutchinson. It stated:

The United States is a beacon of light around the world because of its commitment to human rights. Our government should honor this commitment by recognizing the extreme sexual abuse and violence suffered by Maria Suarez in this country and allow Maria to remain in the U.S. with her family. This is a clear humanitarian case that deserves justice.

Thirty-one members of the U.S. Congress signed it, too.

Maria didn't know how to thank the growing circle of supporters and fighters. She teared up every time Patricia, Jessica, or Charles came to meet with her. It was the first time she knew she could trust again. She had no idea what was going to happen to her next, but she knew she was no longer alone.

> **"** *When I'm free, I will start my own organization, with my own logo: an eagle. The eagle is very powerful. Very smart. Very, very strong. It never backs up from a problem, regardless how bad it is. An eagle can fly through any storm.* **"**

~ Maria Suarez

Wings to Fly

May 24, 2004, was a Monday, and Maria was feeling particularly low that day. Her closest friend had just been deported. Maria was sitting in the dining hall, waiting to go outside for her hour of recreation.

Another detainee was trying to tell Maria some juicy bit of gossip, but Maria was completely distracted. Her eyes kept wandering toward the window where she could just make out a sliver of ocean and sky. She dreamed of floating away to an island or mountaintop. Anywhere that was away from here.

She was lost in thought when a bird flew directly to the window and started tapping on the glass. It was tapping loudly, too, as if to say, *Look up! Over here!*

"Good news!" Maria said out loud. "That bird is bringing me good news!"

The other detainee completely ignored Maria and kept yammering on and on. Maria didn't care. All she could hear was that bird. She knew the bird was trying to tell her something. It fluttered its wings and started tapping again.

"I told you!" Maria squealed. "I'm gonna get good news today. He's bringing me good news!"

The guard let everyone out into the yard for recreation. Maria couldn't find the bird anywhere, but she wasn't panicked. She tried to keep herself busy doing calisthenics and stretches. The fresh air felt alive and hopeful to her.

When she came back in for lunch, she washed her hands and face, filled her tray with salad, and found a little space of bench to sit down. Then she heard the tapping again, only this time it was coming from a different direction. The guard was tapping on the little bubble window from her office.

When Maria looked up, the guard motioned with a single finger, *Come here.*

Maria went into the office. The guard said, "You need to call your attorneys."

"You mean my *attorney*?" Maria asked. "Which one? I have a few."

The guard repeated herself slowly. "Your attorneys."

Maria connected everything right away. She thought of her friend leaving, the bird coming, the word "attorneys." Her body started heating up and trembling.

"Can I please use the phone in the dorm?" Maria whispered. She didn't want to speak too loudly and shatter this incredible moment.

The guard said yes.

Maria called Charles first. She could tell he was trembling, too. He kept on stumbling and stuttering nervously. "Uh, well, uh yeah, I need to tell you something, but Jessica needs to tell you, too."

His fingers fumbled as he tried to connect the three of them in a conference call. Maria was so anxious she felt like she was losing air.

What's going on? Another deportation? Good news? Please somebody say!

Jessica picked up the line.

"Hello!" Maria gasped. And Jessica just started sobbing.

"What is it?" Maria asked.

Jessica said, in between gulps, "You're ... coming ... home!"

May 25, 2004. It was a Tuesday, with intensely open skies. After almost twenty-three years in captivity, and almost six before that locked away with her trafficker, Maria Suarez was finally free.

> **"** It's painful. The pain is never going to go away. But if by me going through the pain, I can help somebody . . . It's my mission, and I need to do it. **"**

~ Maria Suarez

Live, Love, Laugh

Maria wanted to hug everybody. First her family and friends, then complete strangers she saw on the street. The streets, the fresh air, the palm trees all felt so miraculous to her, she didn't know how it could all be here, open and waiting for her.

At the same time, there was something very heavy inside Maria. As she walked into her first day of freedom, she kept feeling like there were weights on her legs, pulling her back, holding her down. She knew her family and her dream team had worked so hard to get her out. She wished she could jump into the celebrations with them. But even as they clinked glasses and turned up her favorite music, Maria was inching toward the door. She had to get someplace quiet to think.

She sat in a lot of cafés and walked miles through parks. The world was so different from what she remembered. She saw a bus stop with slick new benches and posters with movie stars she'd never seen. Young men were wearing baggy jeans and girls had their hair cut up to their ears. Maria cried for all the years she'd lost and all the things she didn't know. She didn't know how to drive. She didn't know how to buy a metro card for the bus. She didn't even know how to use a cell phone.

Her family and friends wanted to help, of course. Her sister insisted that Maria stay with her until she could get her own place. Maria had never been an adult outside of prison. She had all these new skills in computer science and social work, but no idea how or where to apply for a job.

Again, Maria's mom said just a few words that made all the difference.

This time, though, it wasn't about faith. Even though she still sang all the psalms and prayed regularly, Maria's mom couldn't get to church much anymore. She couldn't really take care of herself anymore, either. She was tiny and seemed to be getting smaller each day.

After losing her husband, she'd been diagnosed with Alzheimer's disease and was staying at Maria's sister's place, too. Her words came out jumbled and she often stood with her mouth half open, as if she were caught in the middle of a thought.

One day, Maria found her mom looking through the living room window, studying a neighbor who was mowing his lawn.

"Mommy, what are you looking at?" Maria asked.

Her mom scrunched up her eyebrows and put her tiny hands on her hips.

"That man has a big booty!" she exclaimed.

Maria laughed so hard. It was the first time she remembered laughing like that in forever. She picked up her mom, kissed her, and spun her around. It wasn't poetic or wise, but it was exactly what Maria needed to hear. She needed to be able to look outside and laugh again.

> **❝**

I can get up any time I want to. Eat whatever I want. Move things around. And Just. Be. Me. That's what I like. The freedom to do as I please.

❞ ~ Maria Suarez

Unlocking the Doors

When her mom died, Maria felt like she lost her best friend and lifelong cheerleader. She'd worked and prayed so hard for her freedom, and now that she had it, she lost the one person who meant the most to her. She truly felt her heart aching. She stopped listening to music, or caring about how she looked.

Charles Song, (the lawyer from CAST who'd fought so hard for Maria's release), kept asking her to please come by the CAST offices. When she did, he saw how her face looked shadowed with sadness. He told her he would be her cheerleader now. He also introduced Maria to a network of other survivors and former inmates who were restarting their lives.

Maria was mesmerized by the survivors at CAST who spoke about what they'd been through with such strength and renewed faith in life. She thought she would never want to revisit those days in the old man's house in Azusa. But as she spent more time at the CAST offices, she realized that sharing her past could be liberating not only for her, but also for countless people trying to heal.

The first time Maria tried to describe that house, she didn't know enough words—in English or in Spanish—to express how terrified she was there. She was embarrassed to talk about the bottles on the altar and the voodoo dolls. She waited for people to say *Why didn't you just run?* or *There's no such thing as witches.* But the people at CAST were patient and respectful. They could tell there was much more than a bolted door keeping her in that house. She had been psychologically abused, too. Every day, hearing over and over again how he would kill her family and everyone she loved, beat her into submission.

After Maria started speaking at CAST meetings, she got a call from another anti-trafficking organization called Free the Slaves. They wanted her to be part of their documentary series on former slaves breaking free. As Maria sat, waiting for the camera crew to adjust the lighting and place her microphone, she wondered *Is this really happening to me?*

It was just as real as the moment she lay unconscious in the old man's backyard or when she heard the judge's conviction. It was just as real as when the bird tapped on the window in the prison cafeteria, or when she spun her mom in her arms. It was her new life as an orphaned but strong free woman, unlocking all those closed doors from her past. The more she spoke about what she'd been through, the less power those memories had on her.

She got a job in Los Angeles, counseling victims of domestic violence. She felt so attached to her clients and she admired the way they searched for independence. After each of her group therapy sessions, there was a clump of people waiting to talk to her, wanting one last bit of advice or just one of her warm whispers of *You can do it.*

The invitations kept coming in. Maria's story was featured at anti-trafficking events all over the world. Everyone who met Maria knew immediately that she had an incredible spirit. Her smile took up her whole face, and she smelled like lilac perfume. Her favorite outfit became a black tank top, black pants, and a silver sequined belt and matching pocketbook. And every now and then, she even heard herself hum, or laugh.

> **66**

I think we are all equal. We should treat everybody the same—with love and respect. And value them as who they are. I love white, black, yellow, blue, green, purple, orange... I love people. That's the whole thing—loving people. We don't need to be so cruel.

99

~ Maria Suarez

Peanut Butter Boba

John was waiting for Maria outside the counseling offices again.

"You sure?" he asked as he helped her put on her jacket.

"I'm sure," said Maria. "But, thanks."

"We can just go to city hall and celebrate with peanut butter bobas," John said. This time he held the elevator door for her so she could get in first. He was a gentleman. That much she knew.

"John, I love you, but you know the deal."

"I know, I know," he said. "How about just the bobas then?"

"You're on," Maria said.

Peanut butter bobas were Maria's favorite treat. Bobas are like milkshakes with tapioca balls on the bottom. There was a boba shop just around the corner from the domestic violence counseling center where Maria and John worked together. Maria thought John was hilarious and smart, even a little handsome. And John adored every minute he got to spend with Maria. He asked her to marry him every few days. And even though it stung a little, he understood and respected why she always said no.

Maria was clear that she could never be intimate with a man again after what she'd been through with her abuser. She had no sexual urges or desires anymore. That part of her had entirely shut down. She didn't feel sorry for herself or even lonely. She had a lot of friends, both men and women. She found intimacy in quiet walks or shared meals.

Sitting in the boba shop that afternoon, she squeezed John's hand and said, "This is all I want. Honest."

They each got into their cars and drove home. Maria had a busy evening planned. First, she had to get back to Rialto, where she shared a house with one of her closest friends. Then Maria had to have a tickle fight with her three puppies, Lucky, Princess, and Snuggles. These were her "babies." They wrestled on the floor until each of them was panting.

Maria went for a quick jog around the streets of Rialto. When she got back, she sliced up some cantaloupe, opened a tin of cookies, and put them both on blue plates in the middle of her dining room table. She filled glasses with cool water from her refrigerator. It was important to her that the MSF team was well fueled.

MSF stood for the new Maria Suarez Foundation, dedicated to the prevention of trafficking, and the rescue and restoration of trafficking victims.

Item number one on her agenda for that night's meeting: Maria was thrilled to show the Advisory Board her new certificate of nonprofit status. The board was made up of friends, colleagues, and activists Maria had met in the past few years. They were each incredibly supportive, even though at the last meeting there had been an argument about Maria biting off more than she could chew. Prevention, rescue, and restoration was a lot for a new group to tackle all at once.

But Maria had said it was her vision and she felt passionately about each step. There was no way to do one without the other. *You educate. You get her out. And you empower her with the skills to live a better life.*

Second on the agenda was a presentation from Maria's new art director about logos. Maria had given some input already. She wanted an eagle to be soaring above the letters M, S, and F. Maria loved everything the eagle represented. She never forgot that bird tapping on her window to tell her she'd soon be free.

Item number three was an ongoing challenge: solution-building. This was Maria's mission. This is what made her stomach burn with urgency and purpose. They went around the table and brainstormed new solutions for how to prevent, how to help, how to restore.

At some meetings, everyone had a new idea to offer.

At some meetings, the clock ticking on Maria's stove was the only sound in the room.

At this meeting, Maria held her nonprofit status certificate in one hand and her new eagle logo in the other and said, proudly, "Let's go. Let's do this. Let's make this a better world."

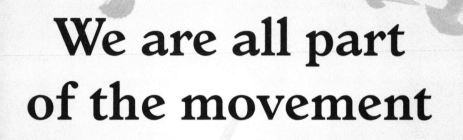

We are all part
of the movement

WHO
...is this happening to?

WHAT
...are we talking about?

WHERE
...is this going on?

WHY
...does this happen?

WHEN
...will we all be truly free?

HOW
...do we break the cycle?

NUMBERS
...we need to know.

NOW
...is the time for action.

WHO
...is this happening to?

"My hope is that young people change their language and the language of their peer group about women in the sex industry. There is a lot of revictimizing the victim and misunderstanding about what kind of 'choice' these women have."
~Rachel Lloyd, Founder and CEO, GEMS

One of the most important things to understand about sex-trafficking survivors is that none of them wanted to go through this. Sometimes it happened to them because someone promised them food or shelter. Sometimes it's because they were born into a society where they're expected to be sexually used and abused. Sometimes it's as simple or familiar as trusting the wrong boyfriend.

Here are just some of the people who are at high risk for sex trafficking.

Runaways
As many as 2.8 million children run away each year in the United States. The National Center for Missing and Exploited Children says that in those first two days of being solo, one out of every three of those children are lured into the sex trade.

One out of every three.

Remember: When someone runs away from home, it's definitely a cry for help. Something at home feels unbearable, and whoever is the first person to promise a better alternative holds all the power, even if what he or she is offering sounds sketchy.

Intergenerational Prostitution
In a lot of places in the world, "tradition" is the excuse used to keep girls and women down. In India, 90 percent of girls born to sex workers are expected to be sold into the sex trade, too. It's their "duty." In societies like this, the boys are brought up to be pimps and the girls are expected to be their prostitutes. The girls can be as young as nine when they're first sold, and their moms can be the ones bringing them to greet their first customers.

Undocumented Immigrants
Immigrants to the United States are super-easy targets for traffickers. When they're new to America, they often don't speak English. Or maybe they don't have a job, they owe money to whoever helped them get here, and they have no legal protection because they're not officially a citizen (yet). The most tragic part of this setup is that immigrants are often trafficked by people from their home country who steer

them the wrong way or promise them an easy ride, and then make them work off their debt by forcing them into the sex trade.

> **"I was impressed by everything about him: his bicycle, his radio, his clothes. When I turned thirteen, he told me he wanted to marry me, and that he could make me a famous singer one day. I agreed."**
> ~ Ayesha, sex-trafficking survivor, Apne Aap

We also have to look carefully at *who* is doing the trafficking. According to the United Nations, 46 percent of victims know their recruiters. Here are some of the faces they wear.

Romeo
The Romeo Pimp is cunning and slick. Once he homes in on his target, he acts like her boyfriend and promises her the world. Romeo tells her she's beautiful and sexy. A lot of times, he buys her expensive presents like cell phones and lingerie that make her feel really special. Then he tells her she's beautiful some more, especially when she puts on lingerie and does a little shimmy. He thinks she's so hot that he wonders if she'll do a little shimmy for his friend. It's just a joke,

he says. Or it's for a special occasion. But this is only the beginning. Romeo has big ideas for her and how beautiful and sexy she can be.

Dutch Loverboy

The loverboy of Holland is a special breed. Since prostitution is legal in the Netherlands if you're eighteen or older, the loverboy preys on underage girls. He pretends to be an adoring boyfriend, doting on his girl with gifts and promises. Soon enough, he starts taking her down to a red light district and telling her this is just something fun they can try, or how it might help to make some money. Sometimes the girls he lures are even forced to work in the windows like sex dolls for sale.

Sex Tourist

Instead of going to see the pyramids in Egypt or surf the waves of Costa Rica, some people travel to another country to buy sex. They might go somewhere where they know the government ignores sexual abuse, where prostitution is legal, or where there is extreme poverty and police corruption. Brazil, Thailand, and the Caribbean islands are hotspot destinations for this kind of customer. Some sex tourists even blog about how many sex workers they have slept with during their travels, and they acquire a reputation as a sort of travel agent and pimp at the same time.

Guerrilla

This is the one who most often makes it into the news. The Guerilla is the guy who lurks in a van or who corners his prey in the public bathroom and uses force to kidnap his victims. A Guerilla will threaten his victim with knives, guns, or the promise that he's going to kill her whole family if she so much as thinks of calling the police. Then he locks her up in his basement or keeps moving her to different locations so nobody can find her. When the Guerilla is finally captured and his victim is freed, a lot of times there are eerie testimonials from neighbors who say something like *I had no idea he had girls in his basement. He was always such a nice, quiet guy.*

WHAT

...are we talking about?

This is a small glossary of terms used by traffickers and survivors of trafficking. When we can all use the same language, we can communicate and hopefully empathize with one another a lot more.

Abolitionist: Anyone who speaks out for freedom and fights for social justice.

AFESIP: Somaly Mam's organization dedicated to rescuing and rehabilitating women who have been trafficked. In French, AFESIP stands for *Agir Pour les Femmes en Situation Précaire,* or, in English, Acting for Women in Distressing Situations.

Bottom: The girl or woman who's been with a pimp/trafficker the longest. Because she knows the ropes, she gets to be a sort of boss's assistant and control the other victims. This can often mean the bottom starts recruiting new girls, too.

Brothel: Any place where people can buy sex. A lot of times brothels are hidden in the back of hotels or cafés. They can also be disguised as spas, massage parlors, bars, strip clubs, or truck stops.

Brujo: The Spanish word for male witch. This word is often associated with witches who practice black magic. Black magic is defined as witchcraft that is used for evil purposes to intentionally harm others, like hexes or curses.

Caste: A division by social class. According to UNICEF, about 250 million people are divided into castes. In a lot of places, your caste determines whom you get to talk to or marry, and also how much money and what kind of jobs and education you can get. Some of the castes in India have intergenerational prostitution as a longstanding tradition.

Coercion: All the ways traffickers keep their victims in the sex trade. Coercion can be verbal, psychological, and/or emotional. Sometimes it's also threats of harm to the victim or victim's family, or threats of deportation and arrest. A lot of times the victim's things are taken away, including phone, keys, and identification, so s/he has no way to contact anyone familiar or reach out for help.

Commercial sex act: Any sex act that includes an exchange of money, food, drugs, shelter, or higher status in a gang. This includes but is not limited to prostitution, exotic dancing, stripping, and pornography.

CPS: Acronym for Child Protective Services, an agency in many states of the U.S. that deals with any reports of child abuse. In some states, CPS goes by another name such as Department of Children and Family Services (DCFS), Department of Social Services (DSS), or Social Services.

CSEC: Acronym for Commercial Sexual Exploitation of Children. CSEC includes but is not limited to prostitution, pornography, sex tourism, and other forms of human trafficking. If the victim is younger than eighteen in the United States, there's no need to show s/he was forced into the situation to be considered a victim of trafficking.

Debt bondage: When a victim is told s/he owes a debt to the trafficker and has to work until it's paid off. Usually there is no limit to what type of work or how long the victim is enslaved. The United Nations calls debt bondage a form of modern-day slavery. It's prevalent in South Asia and India.

Deportation: When a person or group of people is kicked out of a country. This is a common threat used by traffickers of immigrants.

Exploitation: The use of anyone or anything in a cruel way.

Fraud: When a person makes fake promises of love, money, jobs, and a better life so that person can recruit new people into the sex industry.

Green card: An identification card shaped like a driver's license, also known as a **United States Permanent Resident Card.** This card means an immigrant is allowed to live and work in America permanently. It's known as a green card because it's colored green. Anyone who has a green card gets immigration benefits.

Grooming: The way traffickers "break down" or prepare their victims to have sex with strangers. It often involves physical torture, isolation, confiscating the girl's identification, and emotional abuse.

Human trafficking: A crime under federal and international law, also known as **Trafficking In Persons (TIP),** in which the victim is forced or coerced into doing commercial sex acts, labor, or any other service s/he doesn't want to do. Victims do not have to be physically transported anywhere to be trafficked.

Humanitarian: A person who is dedicated to ensuring that all humans are treated justly.

INS: A nickname for United States Citizen and Naturalization Services, which is a division of the U.S. Department of Homeland Security. Previously, similar duties were performed by the U.S. Immigration and Naturalizaton Service, which helped foreign-born people become U.S. citizens and get benefits like Social Security and unemployment. INS detained and/or deported anyone who was illegally living in the United States. After the September 11, 2001 terrorist attacks, the United States reorganized its government agencies and the INS got folded into United States Citizen and Naturalization Services.

Lot lizards: Slang for girls who are forced to prostitute themselves at truck stops and welcome stations.

Meebon: A Cambodian woman who sells girls into the sex trade. *Meebons* are in charge of feeding, clothing, and housing the girls. They usually add up all these expenses and tell the girls they are paying off a debt. Every night the *meebons* rent girls out to as many clients as possible.

Modern-day slavery/Modern slavery: Another way to describe human trafficking. Free the Slaves estimates there are 27 million people being trafficked today, meaning people being recruited, transported, and forced into servitude. They may not wear shackles or be branded with their pimp's name on their necks, but they are slaves.

Recruiter: Anyone who finds and recruits people into the trafficking network.

Pimp: Anyone who controls or coerces someone else to perform sex acts for paying customers. The pimp keeps all the profits.

Pimps up, ho's down: Slang for the physical location of a pimp and the girl he is selling. The pimp always has to be somehow above the girl; for instance, if he's standing on the sidewalk, she has to stand in the street. There are also rules about when and how she can make eye contact with her pimp. She can *never* make eye contact with another pimp, or else she'll get in serious trouble.

Prostitute: Someone who receives money for sex, or, when used as a verb, to use someone or something disrespectfully, especially to make money. Traffickers prostitute their victims.

Quota: The dollar amount that a pimp sets for his girls each night. If a girl doesn't earn as much as her quota, she is sent back out onto the street or she's severely punished. Everything she earns goes to the pimp. *Everything.*

Re-naming: A way of erasing a victim's true identity. When a pimp gives his girls nicknames, it may seem cute or affectionate but that's not why he does it. It's part of a power play to eliminate her past.

Safe harbor laws: State laws that are intended to help sexually exploited children. In 2008, California and New York State both signed Safe Harbor laws after years of advocacy to get state legislators to see that children in prostitution are not criminals or delinquents, but instead are victims of abuse who need special services like counseling, safe houses, protection, and education.

Sex trafficking: The act of forcing, coercing, or conning someone into performing any sexual act. According to U.S. law, anyone younger than eighteen years old who is selling or being sold for sex acts is a victim of sex trafficking, whether it's done by force or not.

Square: Anyone who tries to get out of the trafficking system or people who try to help others get out.

Stockholm Syndrome: A common psychological reaction to being held captive or abused. Victims get numb from all the beatings, become scared that there is nothing else out there, and, most of all, feel incredibly *loyal* to their abuser. They will defend their abuser and fight off anyone who tries to help them leave. This is yet another reason why it's so hard to get victims out of a horrible situation. They are often traumatized and psychologically dependent on their abusers.

Survivor leadership: When people who have freed themselves from trafficking choose to speak out about their stories, lead awareness and recovery efforts, or go before legislators to talk about what they've been through and advocate for legal changes.

Swedish model of prosecution: Convicting men who pay for sex of a crime, instead of jailing the women as prostitutes. In 1999, the Swedish government changed its laws to ensure that women are treated as victims instead of criminals. This was a revolutionary move, and many governments and activists agree it's been a huge milestone in fighting sex trafficking.

The Track (a.k.a. the stroll): The street corners or other areas where it's known that prostitutes can stand and get paid for sex each night.

Trafficking Victims Protection Act (TVPA): The first U.S. government act signed into law to define human trafficking and name clear consequences for anyone accused of being a trafficker. The TVPA, adopted in 2000, defines sex trafficking as "the recruitment, harboring, transportation, provision, or obtaining of a person for the purpose of a commercial sex act where such an act is induced by force, fraud, or coercion, or in which the person induced to perform such an act has not attained eighteen years of age."

In other words, anyone forced or conned into the sex industry is a victim. And if that somebody is younger than eighteen, s/he doesn't need proof of being forced—which is a hard thing to prove anyway. People found guilty of sex trafficking can be sentenced to as much as life imprisonment. The TVPA was reauthorized in 2003, 2005, and 2008.

Transition age youth: People between the ages of eighteen and twenty-five. This is viewed as a significant time in people's lives because the brain becomes fully developed.

Tricks (a.k.a. dates or johns): Anyone who buys commercial sex.

Wife in Law (a.k.a. family or folks): Each woman or girl who is being bought, sold, and controlled by the same pimp.

WHERE

...is this going on?

"We need to keep our eyes open. We need to stay
vigilant, and we need to realize that this can
appear in almost any industry [...] there's been
a case of elder care workers in a nursing home.
There's been a case of golf course groundskeepers
in a fancy golf course. There have been cases in
the fishing industry and nail salons and
restaurants, all these different places where we
need to stay vigilant."

~Bradley Myles,
CEO of Polaris Project, on NPR

Human trafficking means someone is forced or coerced
into doing commercial sex acts, labor, or any other service s/he doesn't want to do. It is a global and hard-to-
detect epidemic. Sad but true: You can close your eyes,
point to any place on a world map, and you're going
to learn that there's some form of human trafficking
there, too.

There are more people trafficked and held captive as slaves today than there were over the course
of the transatlantic slave trade. Every year, between
700,000 and 4 million women and children are trafficked, most often in the sex trade. Some of the biggest

hubs for human trafficking are Algeria, Central African Republic, China, Cuba, Iran, North Korea, Kuwait, Libya, Mauritania, Papua New Guinea, Saudi Arabia, Sudan, Syria, Yemen, and Zimbabwe, according to the Trafficking in Persons Report issued by the U.S. Department of State. The more we can do to become aware, the more we can stop trafficking from spreading.

Here are just a few more places where sex trafficking is all too common:

Minnesota Pipeline

There are some estimates that Minnesota has as many as ten thousand people being trafficked there. It's been nicknamed the Minnesota Pipeline because of its reputation as a place where young girls can easily be lured into trafficking. In 2008, the Federal Bureau of Investigation declared Minneapolis the eighth worst city in the United States for trafficking of juveniles. Maybe even worse than those numbers, is that the typical age of girls being trafficked in Minnesota is between eleven and fourteen.

The French Parliament

No, people are not being exploited in the Senate, but it is where some of the biggest decisions are being made about how to end trafficking. The government of France says there are about twenty thousand people in France's commercial sex trade, and about 75 percent are forced into it. There are also (too) many children sold into the French sex industry, mostly from Romania, West Africa, and North Africa. Now, France's Senate is trying to decide whether to follow the Swedish model of prosecution, in which the people who buy sex are prosecuted and fined. A lot of countries in Europe are trying to decide whether or not to do the same.

The Philippines

A major storm can bring havoc to any location. The aftermath of a tornado or a hurricane not only leads to loss of life and property, but there is often a big spike in human trafficking in the affected areas. Children who lose their parents in the disaster, or adults who are desperate for work, are picked up by a "family friend" or "aid relief." And while natural disasters can happen anywhere, when Typhoon Haiyan hit the Philippines in 2013, the nation saw a significant increase in sex trafficking. The city of Olongapo in the Philippines, in particular, now has a bustling red light district, and there are already welfare agencies trying to find out who brought children from the site of the typhoon to this city.

Uttari Rampur Red Light Area, India

India is the country with the most people enslaved in the world. Between 13,300,000 and 14,700,000 people are currently forced into all types of slavery. The Uttari Rampur Red Light district is one area where women and girls are forced into sexual slavery. A pimp—who who could easily be the new husband a young girl was forced to marry—locks her up for five years and sells her each night to different customers. After the first five years, she's allowed to "keep" half of what she earns. But really, the brothel takes money for rent for the bed, her makeup, her medical bills, and her food. Again, she winds up with less than nothing. Plus, she was never allowed to go to school, so how could she possibly count her money even if it was in her hands? The rest of her life is about paying off this "debt" that the pimp says she owes him.

Intercontinental Hotel, Qingdao, China

The Intercontinental Hotel in Qingdao, China, is a hotspot for sex tourists, but there are many other hotels nearby offering "special massages." Hotels like this exist all over the world, and sometimes even the hotel owners don't know what's being sold because the spa is run by another management company (a.k.a. the pimp). There are between four million and six million sex workers in China. Many of them work in places that say they are barbers' shops, massage parlors, or karaoke bars. People also are trafficked into forced marriages, especially in rural areas. In 2010, there were at least 122 cases of women being trafficked from Myanmar to China and then sold into a forced marriage.

Port Authority Bus Terminal (PABT), New York City

Port Authority is the hub for interstate buses into New York City. It's in midtown Manhattan, just one block west of Times Square. It has about eight thousand buses and a quarter-million people going through it on an average weekday, totaling more than 65 million people a year. A lot of these are young people who don't know where to go and who are easily persuaded by a helpful-looking older man, one who says he knows the way home, or asks if maybe she wants to join him for a drink before she gets back on the bus.

WHY

...does this happen?

"Whenever I told him I was going to leave, he'd recite the address of my little sister's daycare."

~Anonymous survivor

When we talk about why this happens, it's a lot about the lack of choice. Some people have the crazy idea that victims of sex trafficking have a choice. Really? What kind of choices do you have as a ten-year-old? A fifteen-year-old? Even a twenty-year-old? Biologically, the human brain isn't fully developed until about age twenty-five. We don't let people drink or drive or vote before late teens, early twenties. So the answer to why this happens is because sex trafficking victims have no other choice.

If someone they trust and love says, "Hey, you're so beautiful. I want you to dance for my friend. It'll make you feel good," it makes sense that they'd give it a shot.

Or if one of their parents says, "You have to help out the family or we'll have nothing to eat." There's not really a choice here, is there?

And whenever physical abuse and rape is added to that, all choice is completely lost. There is only fear of it happening again. There is a big *or else* hanging over their every move.

According to a New York City law enforcement official, this was one trafficker's way of scouting out who would be the next girl he pimped:

"I walk through the mall and say, 'You're very pretty,' and if the girl looks me in the eye and says, 'Thanks,' then I know to keep walking. If she looks down and says, 'No, I'm not' then I know she's the one I'm gonna get."

Traffickers come in all shapes and sizes. The thing they all have in common is that they know how to find their victims' most vulnerable spots, tricking them with false promises or beating them into submission.

Traffickers are also very smart and savvy. They are expert mind manipulators. Whether it's erasing all her cell phone contacts so she's completely isolated or telling her he will kill her family if she breathes a word about him, he has a hold on his victim's psyche. He figures out exactly what she is scared of or feeling insecure about and digs in. There are so many ways physically and psychologically that traffickers keep their victims caught in the system. Here are just a few.

Low Self-Esteem
This one is universal. We all go through bouts of self-doubt, wondering where we fit in. Especially as teens

when everything starts to change—our friends, our bodies, our hormones. Adolescence is a hugely vulnerable time. When someone points to you and says you look pretty or he believes in you, it feels only natural to be attracted to that kind of attention. This is just one way in which traffickers are mind manipulators.

Physical Abuse and Threats

It is common that victims are abused physically in some way while being held captive. Some are knocked unconscious by their beatings on a regular basis. Traffickers often promise that they will kill their victim and/or the victim's family if s/he tries to run away or call anyone for help.

Deportation

A lot of trafficking victims are from foreign countries, so deportation is a terrifying threat for them. Traffickers steal identification and green cards, cell phones, and any other identifying objects. They also often have a mob of conspirators back in the victim's home country ready to "greet" her if she's sent back home. Not to mention that she may not even speak English and could be completely in the dark about where she's located.

Constant Relocation

This is another common tactic for traffickers. They

move around a country quickly and secretively. This means the victims never know exactly what city or state they'll wake up in the next morning, law enforcement cannot track them down, and the victims cannot get familiarized or find out where safe houses are. Each new city could mean different names or identifications for victims, too. Pretty soon, the girls cannot tell who, what, or where they are, and they're completely isolated from family or friends who could possibly get them out.

Criminal Charges

If you are a victim and you try to call the authorities, what will happen? Even though victims of sex trafficking have been horrifically abused, many times if they try to contact law enforcement, they can be charged with prostitution, indecent exposure, or loitering. Anyone being trafficked who's older than eighteen has to prove "force, fraud, and coercion," which is very hard. A lot of people (jurors, lawyers, even judges) still don't understand that prostitutes are most often victims instead of culprits. If you're charged with prostitution, you could be sentenced to many months in jail and required to pay fines, which vary from state to state. If you're younger than eighteen and brought into foster care (a common "solution"), you never know what kind of family you'll be placed in. Plus, once you turn eighteen, you're put back on the street because you've "aged out," which means the government says you're too old to need a guardian.

Cults

It feels good to be part of a secret club, especially when the leader tells you that you've found your calling and are on your way to a new, carefree existence. Cults are religious groups of people who follow one leader, often isolating themselves so they can devote themselves fully. Cult leaders recruit people through all sorts of tactics, often promising psychological or spiritual miracles. And once there is a small group on board with the cult's mission, each member starts recruiting new people to come into the fold. Not all cults are involved in sex trafficking, but there are some significant and scary cases involving child marriages, sexual servitude, and mass suicide. Victims in these situations are often lured by the leader of the cult who builds a strong, trusting relationship with them, and then asks them to prove their faith.

Stockholm Syndrome

If you've never experienced abuse or coercion, this could be hard to understand, but Stockholm Syndrome is very real and very powerful. People who develop Stockholm Syndrome will defend their abusers and traffickers no matter what. If anyone asks them whether they chose to be a sex worker or were trafficked, they will say it was their choice. Why? Because there is a psychological hold that traffickers have on their victims. A lot of people call it brainwashing.

Think about it: The trafficker has convinced his victim that she's the love of his life. Or that he wants to start a family with her. If he's been violent, he swears he's going to change and he wants to be good for her. Or he tells her that as soon as they make the next rent check he won't make her work anymore. And she believes him. Because no matter how horrible he's been to her, he's also the one who found her when she was completely lost. He's the only one to praise her and tell her that she's beautiful. Maybe he's even her father. So yes, he has control over her sense of reason and, in some cases, this is what keeps her there night after night.

**"We, the bystanders, have had to look within ourselves to find some small portion of the courage that victims of violence must muster every day."
~ Dr. Judith Herman, author of *Trauma and Recovery***

WHY do we still put up with this happening all over the world?

There's really no answer for this question. In every nation there will be a different "reason" or, really, "excuse" for why people are still being bought and sold for sex. In some places, it's part of an age-old tradition. In others, it's more of a subtle psychological game.

WHY is prostitution and pimp daddy language still glamorized in American music and pop culture?

There are too many songs about the "glory" of pimping to list them all in one book. Seriously. Rap and hip-hop artists sing about pimping as if they are doing "their girls" a favor and the world should cheer for them. Here's just a sampling of the songs I've found that have the scariest lyrics:

- **"Pimpin' All Over the World"** by Ludacris
- **"Pimp"** by 8Ball & Mjg
- **"P.I.M.P."** by 50 Cent
- **"Pimp"** by Trick Daddy
- **"Hard Out Here for a Pimp"** by Three 6 Mafia

And what about all the video games where kids are taught that pimpin' is silly and fun? **"Grand Theft Auto," "Ho-Tel,"** and **"Second Life"** are just a handful of horrible activities you can find.

Please, instead of visiting these sites and getting hurt and furious, check out Wicked Evolution's anti-trafficking

music video with Jada Pinkett Smith singing "Nada."
www.youtube.com/watch?v=G_SdBiTIocA

WHY is prostitution legal
in the Netherlands?

In 2000, the Netherlands made prostitution legal. The idea was that the government could give health care to sex workers and cut down on trafficking. So far, this experiment has done mostly the opposite. Yes, there are more health checkups in brothels, but that doesn't mean sexually transmitted diseases or HIV have faded. Trafficking and forced prostitution are still popular, and because people know they can't be arrested for visiting brothels, the sex industry is booming.

WHY do patrol guards in India stop
people from smuggling in pirated DVDs
but not Nepali girls?

Nepali girls aren't "worth" as much as a DVD. In many parts of India, it's an unspoken rule that young men cannot sleep with their girlfriends until marriage. This is said to make them angry and sexually frustrated. So peasant girls are shipped in from Nepal to Kolkata. One border guard described it as a way to keep the peace.

WHY are Yemeni girls as young as ten forced into "marriages" where the men are decades older and often violent?

The parliament of Yemen still refuses to ban child marriages or at least set a minimum age for girls to get married. The United Nations and many other human rights organizations are trying to change this, but until the Yemeni government listens, there are many girls in danger. Some of them die during childbirth or even during sex because they are so young and treated so violently. Sometimes they're being trafficked and married to their own cousins.

WHY does Sweden have the right idea?

The Swedish model of prosecution, which was started in 1999, means that in Sweden, Norway, and Iceland, the people who buy sex are punished instead of the people being sold. Since 1999, street prostitution and sex trafficking have both decreased significantly in these countries. So now the question is, Why isn't the rest of the world getting on board with this idea?

WHEN

...will we all be truly free?

**"I hope that someday people don't have to
celebrate their anniversary of freedom.
I hope that everyone's freedom date will
forever and always be their birth date."**

~Minh Dang

These are just a handful of moments that are significant in the anti-trafficking movement. It's crazy to see that even while we pass laws that "free" people, slaves remain. Feel free to write your own timeline with moments when you felt empowered or stood up for freedom. Then see how our stories are all connected.

1863: U.S. President Abraham Lincoln signs the **Emancipation Proclamation,** which commands all rebel states to free their slaves.

1910: The Mann Act is passed as a federal law. Also known as the White Slave Traffic Act, this makes it illegal in the United States to take women across state lines for consensual sex. It also makes it a felony to coerce a woman or a girl into prostitution, debauchery, or any other "immoral acts."

1948: The United Nations General Assembly adopts the Universal Declaration of Human Rights, which bans slavery globally.

1974: The Child Abuse Prevention and Treatment Act (CAPTA) is enacted to protect children from abuse legally in the United States.
(Note: The federal Animal Welfare Act was passed eight years earlier in the United States.)

1976: Maria Suarez comes to America with her sister and father. When Maria goes on a job interview, she is locked up and abused, becoming a sex slave for almost six years.

1981: Maria Suarez is charged with conspiracy to murder her trafficker and sent to prison.

1989: The United Nations General Assembly adopts The Convention on the Rights of the Child, which is an international law that is supposed to protect the rights of anyone under eighteen years old.

1991: Somaly Mam refuses to be bought or sold for sex ever again.

1996: Somaly Mam starts *Agir Pour les Femmes en Situation Précaire* (AFESIP) to rescue and restore victims of sexual exploitation. She opens AFESIP's first shelter the following year.

1998: Rachel Lloyd, trafficking survivor and activist, opens Girls Educational & Mentoring Services (GEMS)—the only organization in New York state created for girls and young women who've been through commercial sexual exploitation and domestic trafficking. When she starts GEMS (out of her apartment), Rachel has $30, a laptop, and a hunger to change the world.

2000: The Trafficking Victims Protection Act (TVPA) is passed in the United States. It defines human trafficking and the penalties for anyone convicted of trafficking. It is re-authorized in **2003, 2005,** and **2008** with the help of survivors speaking before legislators and demanding to be heard.

2003: California Governor Arnold Schwarzenegger grants Maria Suarez parole on December 16 (and sends her straight to an Immigration and Naturalization detention center).

2004: CAST opens the first and only shelter in the United States exclusively for survivors of trafficking.

2004: On May 25, Maria Suarez is released from INS detention and declared officially free.

2005: The first time Minh Dang says no to her father raping her. "It was kinda the first time I said no in general to anything he asked me to do. That night, my mom had left him and he asked me to return home to stay with him. And I said, 'No.'"

2006: The Department of Justice reports that 1,600 children are arrested for prostitution and commercialized vice (even though the TVPA is supposed to stop punishing any child caught in the trafficking system).

2006: On April 14, Minh Dang tells her parents that she will no longer sell her body for them and that if they try to contact her she will alert the police.

2007: Somaly Mam teams up with Jared Greenberg and Nicholas Lumpp to start the Somaly Mam Foundation. SMF is part of Somaly's vision to "expand and improve victim services, to prevent trafficking with grassroots advocacy and education, and to provide a platform for the survivor voice to be heard around the world."

2008: The Safe Harbor Act is passed in New York and California, helping children who've been trafficked get protective services and counseling instead of being treated as criminals.

2013: With the help of Equality Now survivors, the New York Safe Harbor Act is extended to protect persons less than eighteen years old from being treated like a criminal after they've been trafficked.

2013: The Federal Bureau of Investigation, other law enforcement agencies, and the National Center for Missing and Exploited Children (NCMEC) conduct Operation Cross Country VII. They recover more than a hundred children who have been trafficked for sex. There are also nearly one hundred sixty pimps arrested on state and federal charges.

HOW

... do we break the cycle?

More and more incredible organizations each day are reaching out and helping victims of sex trafficking. Many of the brave survivors, legislators, and counselors in this book are either founders or active members of these groups.

Apne Aap
www.apneaap.org
In Hindi, Apne Aap means "self-empowerment." Apne Aap was founded by a journalist named Ruchira Gupta and twenty-two women from Mumbai's red light district. Apne Aap creates self-empowerment groups for women so they can gain independence and have new choices in education, jobs, safe housing, and legal protection. Since 2002, Apne Aap has helped more than fifteen thousand women across India. Now they're taking their mission worldwide.

Breaking Free
www.breakingfree.net
Breaking Free, whose motto is "Sisters Helping Sisters Break Free," was started by a brilliant survivor named Vednita Carter. She is dedicated to helping women and girls break free from prostitution and sexual exploita-

tion through advocacy, direct services, housing, and education. Her team goes onto the streets in Minneapolis and St. Paul, Minnesota, spreading the word that there is a safe place to go.

CAST (Coalition to Abolish Slavery & Trafficking)
www.castla.org
CAST offers shelter, food, supportive counseling, and critical legal services to trafficking victims nationwide. It also runs a toll-free hotline. Its Caucus of Survivors travels to speak out on behalf of all survivors. **MARIA SUAREZ** met the lawyers who helped her out of prison through CAST.

Children of the Night
www.childrenofthenight.org
Children of the Night is dedicated to ending child prostitution. It runs a home with an on-site school and college placement program. Caseworkers follow up with graduates, too. The Children of the Night hotline is ready and able to rescue children twenty-four hours a day, and it provides transportation to the home nationwide.

Courtney's House
www.courtneyshouse.org
Courtney's House is a survivor-led organization that is on the front lines of the anti-trafficking movement. Every Friday and Saturday night, the Courtney's House

team hits the streets of Washington, D.C., looking for potential victims and (secretly) passing out the hotline number for help. Courtney's House has already helped more than five hundred victims escape trafficking.

Don't Sell Bodies
www.dontsellbodies.org

This website was started by the Will and Jada Smith Family Foundation "to raise awareness about domestic human trafficking, to inspire public action, and to empower survivor voices." The site offers facts, figures, and stories from survivors and news of any and all changes in the anti-trafficking movement. It also has links, hotlines, and many ways of offering help to people who fear they may be in danger.

ECPAT (End Child Prostitution, Child Pornography & Trafficking of Children for Sexual Purposes)
www.ecpatusa.org

ECPAT tackles the Commercial Sexual Exploitation of Children (CSEC) worldwide. It has a ton of different campaigns to raise awareness, following which governments are doing what to end CSEC, advocating for victims, and developing new legislation that protects victims and penalizes traffickers and exploiters. It also helps caregivers to make the rescue and recovery process smoother.

Equality Now
www.equalitynow.org
"Ending violence and discrimination against women and girls around the world" is the motto of Equality Now, which works with survivors and lawyers to change anti-trafficking laws. Its members passionately believe we must criminalize traffickers and buyers of sex and decriminalize victims. Equality Now also works with survivors to rehabilitate and advocate for change worldwide.

FAIR Girls
www.fairgirls.org
FAIR stands for Free, Aware, Inspired, and Restored. FAIR believes these are adjectives that should describe every girl. FAIR Girls has programs in Bosnia, Montenegro, Serbia, Russia, Uganda, and the United States. In Washington, D.C., (its home office) Fair Girls offers emergency response for victims, individual counseling, group empowerment workshops, and educational outreach about trafficking prevention.

Half The Sky: Turning Oppression into Opportunity For Women Worldwide
www.halftheskymovement.org
It started as an incredible book about survivors like Somaly Mam and the work they are doing around the

world to free and inspire women. Then came a phenomenal documentary about these women. Now, Half the Sky has expanded into a global movement. You can go online to find out all the different ways to get involved: supporting individual survivors, sharing stories, volunteering, or even playing a Facebook Half the Sky game about worldwide emancipation.

GEMS (Girls Educational & Mentoring Services)
www.gems-girls.org
Created and led by abolitionist and survivor **Rachel Lloyd**, GEMS empowers young women across America to break out of the trafficking and sex industry and develop to their full potential. You can see many of the champions of GEMS in the movie *Very Young Girls*, which shows the ugly truth about the commercial sexual exploitation of girls in New York City.

Polaris Project
www.polarisproject.org
Polaris works on all levels of the anti-trafficking movement. It has social services for victims in its local offices (Washington, D.C., and New Jersey). It also constantly works on state and federal policies with government officials to help protect victims and prosecute traffickers. It operates the central twenty-four-hour national human trafficking hotline for the

United States and plans to make it an international hotline network by 2020.

The SAGE Project (Standing Against Global Exploitation)

www.sagesf.org

The SAGE Project's mission is "to improve the lives of persons who have experienced or are at risk of sexual exploitation, human trafficking, violence, and other forms of trauma." It offers counseling, case management, mental health therapy, process groups, holistic healing, and advocacy internationally. Its members specifically speak out about the demand for sexual exploitation, and help train people who work with survivors.

Somaly Mam Foundation

www.somaly.org

In many ways the inspiration for this book, Somaly Mam's foundation is "dedicated to the eradication of slavery and the empowerment of its survivors." Whether it's speaking in front of government officials, training survivors to speak out with her, or creating beautiful crafts in the Empowerment Store, Somaly and her team are always thinking of new and creative ways to help survivors and end human trafficking worldwide once and for all.

NUMBERS

...we need to know.

Statistics on human trafficking are, at best, guessti-
mates because this crime is secretive and we are still
creating better ways to detect and prevent it.

STATISTIC:

The United Nations reports that almost **two million**
people are trafficked each year into the sex trade. On
any given night in New York, more than **four thousand** underage youth are trafficked for sex.

NUMBER TO CALL:

National Trafficking Hotline: 1-888-373-7888
This hotline can help you find community resources
or sound out whether you know someone who's being
trafficked—including yourself.

STATISTIC:

The U.S. Department of Justice says the number of
children (under eighteen years old) caught in commercial sexual exploitation is **between 100,000 and three
million.**

NUMBER TO CALL:

CAST hotline: 1-888-KEY-2-FREEDOM (888-539-2373)

Run by the Coalition to Abolish Slavery & Trafficking, this is a number you can call if you suspect or have experienced human trafficking, or if you want to learn more about CAST and how you can get involved.

STATISTIC:
The average age of people entering the U.S. commercial sex industry is **twelve to fourteen years old.**

NUMBER TO CALL:
Children of the Night Hotline: 1-800-551-1300
The Children of the Night hotline is open twenty-four hours a day. Children of the Night gives free taxi and airline transportation nationwide for America's child prostitutes who want to live in the home. Hotline staff members work with law enforcement officials to rescue children safely and effectively.

STATISTIC:
Reebok gave rap star 50 Cent a **$50 million** sneaker endorsement deal after his song "P.I.M.P.," which glamorizes pimping, went platinum.

NUMBER TO CALL:
Survivor-By-Survivor Hotline: 1-888-261-3665
This hotline is provided by Courtney's House and run by survivors, for survivors. The phone is answered by

people who know what it's like and want to help you or anyone you think may be being prostituted.

STATISTICS:

In 2012 in Kolkata, India, Apne Aap helped get **814 children** into schools, and this past year it also enrolled the first girls ever from the Nat caste into college! Nat caste is a very poor group of people from North India.

In 2012 in Cambodia, over **1,200 women and girls** visited Somaly Mam's free medical clinic for consultations, counseling, and treatment. **Eighteen women and girls** who visited were able to get out of their trafficking situation and enroll in an AFESIP recovery center.

In 2013 in Albany, New York, Equality Now brought **three survivors** to testify before state legislators. As a result, the Safe Harbor law was extended to cover *all* prostituted individuals under the age of eighteen in New York. Thanks to these bold survivors, sixteen- and seventeen-year-old victims who are arrested for prostitution will be classified as victims and given treatment services instead of going to jail. Their criminal records will also be sealed.

NUMBER TO CALL:
Yourself

Okay, that's a little hard to do unless you have two phones. But you can write yourself a note. Thank yourself for being strong, honest, passionate, and alive. Make a promise always to look out for yourself and be true to yourself no matter what tomorrow brings. You can also call your best friend and share this pact.

NOW

…is the time for action.

**"Even if you're just talking about it to
a friend, it's raising awareness. It has to
start with us questioning the norm."**
~Anita Channapati, former
special victims and sex crimes
prosecutor in New York City

Once you hear these courageous voices, you can't unhear them. So what can *you* do right now to join the anti-trafficking movement?

Start with a deep breath, a conversation. Close your eyes, open them again, and see the world with new eyes. Or start with reading this book. Maybe share it with a friend. It's that simple and huge at the same time.

The more this is talked about, the stronger we become. It's not about living in fear. It's about being aware and becoming involved when we can.

Sounds easy, right? But in a lot of ways, it's easier to send a donation to a charity halfway around the globe because then you don't have to see whom it's affecting or the faces that need you.

So here are just a few ideas for how we can all be part of the anti-trafficking movement, if we choose to be. Most important, please go slowly. Don't make any promises you can't keep or feel like you must see immediate change. It's a revolution that's been building for centuries. Find a way to support your own freedom and your sisters' at the same time.

Read.

Here are a handful of books by survivors and activists in the anti-trafficking movement that are incredible. The strength of their voices will draw you into each page.

Girls Like Us: Fighting for a World Where Girls Are Not for Sale (a memoir)
by Rachel Lloyd

The Road of Lost Innocence: The True Story of a Cambodian Heroine
by Somaly Mam

Half the Sky: Turning Oppression into Opportunity for Women Worldwide
by Nicholas D. Kristof and Sheryl WuDunn

Radhika's Story: Surviving Human Trafficking
by Sharon Hendry and Joanna Lumley

Write.

Do you know any people in politics? Journalists or community leaders? Well, get to know them.

Write to Craigslist and tell them they have to stop allowing people to be sold on their site. Write to your elected officials. Tell them what you know about trafficking and that you want stronger laws to protect victims. You can get news from Polaris Project, Equality Now, or Don't Sell Bodies about whom to write and which laws we need to pass for greater protections.

Write to newspapers, magazines, and television stations to publish stories about modern-day slavery, and how to stop it.

You can write to the president of the United States if you feel the urge. You'll never know the power of your words until you try.

Talk.

To anyone you think will listen. Talk to friends who you think may be at risk in any way—problems at home, a controlling boyfriend, or maybe she's just really into showing off her body in a way that scares you. Start a group at your school to talk about how you can motivate people and treat one another with respect. Talk to trusted counselors and mentors about anything suspicious you see or call one of the hotlines listed in the "Numbers" section of this book to talk about these issues with trained professionals.

Volunteer.

With any of the organizations (listed in "How") who are caring for survivors. Help build shelters or teach English. Be part of a skills training group. Maybe you love cooking or kick boxing. Ask if you can lead a workshop. Walk into any organization or call and ask how you can best lend a hand.

Be cool, man.

This book is mostly about the girls and women affected by sex trafficking, but of course we need to look at the demand for sex and the way boys are taught that pimping is "hot." Apne Aap has a great "Cool Men Don't Buy Sex" campaign. Visit the Apne Aap website to see how you can start a "Cool Men" movement: *www.apneaap.org/cmdbs/cool-men-dont-buy-sex-campaign.*

Shop!

You can buy jewelry and gifts made by survivors. It is incredibly empowering to survivors to learn a new skill like jewelry making or sewing, especially as they are healing from trauma. Each piece of cloth or bead is filled with hope and new light. Whether you wear it yourself or give it to someone else, you're helping to expand the anti-trafficking momentum. Look at the beautiful gifts being made here:

International Sanctuary, Purchase with Purpose
Jewelry, stationery, awesome gifts for kids and adults
www.isanctuary.org

Made By Survivors
Jewelry, bags, the cutest backpacks you'll ever carry
www.madebysurvivors.com

Somaly's Empowerment Store
Cards, jewelry, clothing, accessories, inspiring books and CDs
www.empowermentstore.org

Oh, and perhaps the most important thing you CAN and MUST do NOW:

**"Practice and cultivate self-love...
Empowering survivors to be who they
are is really the same as empowering
anyone to be themselves."**
~Minh Dang

Afterword

The same old street, but with a new door

This morning, I was riding my bicycle to the local public pool in Brooklyn. It was a little past sunrise and the streets were familiar to me. But I saw something I'd never seen before.

The flash and glitter of a tall woman wearing a black skin-tight spandex outfit and stilettos caught my eye. She looked like she was about twenty years old—maybe younger. She was walking quickly along the broken sidewalk. Then a thick metal door opened up out of a brick warehouse-looking building. I saw a man's stocky arm holding the door open. The edge of his T-shirt was a faded red and stained. As the woman rushed in, the stocky arm shut the door swiftly behind her.

I saw this for the first time today, even though I've been down this old street before. It's not far from my apartment. Not far from the local coffee shop where I often sit for hours and write. Not far from the playground where I bring my kids to swing and splash in the sprinklers.

I saw this just today, and I wanted to stop my bicycle, sit on that broken sidewalk, and weep.

But I'm the one making up the rest of this woman's story. I don't know who she is or what she was doing. I certainly don't know if she's being trafficked. Maybe she was going into an unmarked door just after dawn dressed the way she was dressed for a gazillion reasons. Wouldn't it be great if she were getting home from a disco party with her closest friends that went all night, or even a masquerade?

Whatever her story is, I owe it to her to stop and think. Just as I owe it to the extraordinary girls and women in this book who walked into unmarked doors that changed their lives forever. Their voices fill me with tremendous hope, and also a great sense of responsibility.

So today, right now, I have a choice to make.

I can look up the address of that building and call any organization I trust to report what I saw, making sure I contact people who won't put that girl in any danger.

I can volunteer at the teen shelter near my apartment and get to know my neighbors more honestly.

I can write a letter to our new mayor and ask him exactly how buyers of sex are being prosecuted.

I can talk to friends about this door and ask if they've seen it, too.

Whatever I decide, I have to do *something*.

It's the same old street I know so well. Only, now I see it with new eyes.

I see how it's my chance to help one more person break free.

Acknowledgments

There are so many incredible people who helped make this book possible. Thank you to Jen Zeigler who led me to the incredible NoVo Foundation. Thank you to Jody Myrum, Caitlin Ho, and Pamela Shifman at the NoVo Foundation; Megan and Melissa at Gracehaven; Rachel Lloyd and Twanna at GEMS; Ruchira Gupta, Lindsey Swedick, Tinku Khanna, Sahana Dasgupta, and Anupam Das at Apne Aap; Anita Channapati; Vednita Carter of Breaking Free; and Lauren Hersh from Equality Now. Your patience, wisdom, and encouragement have been such gifts to me.

Thank you to Ben Skinner, Nicholas Kristof, and Sheryl WuDunn for your inspirational writing on human trafficking and for cracking open worlds that were secret for so long.

Thank you to Amy Klein, Kimmi Berlin, and Judy Batalion for reading and re-reading my words, making sense of my half-baked ideas. To Emma Tsui, Kim Thackeray, Gabra Zackman, Megan Grano, Sara Moss, Alexander London, Joselin Linder, and Alysia Reiner for constantly motivating me and buying me coffee.

Thank you to Lori Black, Abigail Disney, and Leymah Gbowee, who taught me the importance of standing up to make a difference. Thank you to my dear friend Samantha Mary Karpel, who was the first person to teach me that my voice could matter.

Thank you to my amazingly kind and supportive agent, Joelle Delbourgo. Thank you to the entire Barron's team, especially my awesomely inspiring editor, Angela Tartaro.

Thank you, thank you to my incredibly loving family; Betsy, Jon, Easy, Boppy, and CK; Jason, Sunny, and Zev, who told me all the time that I could do it and reminded me every day to enjoy knock-knock jokes. An extra special thank you to Samson Bird, who grew in my belly as this book was born and is already teaching me so much about seeing the world anew.

And of course, thank you to the generous, extraordinary survivors who spoke to me about their experiences. J.K. Rowling once said, "The truth. It is a beautiful and terrible thing, and must therefore be treated with great caution."

Thank you so much for entrusting me with your truth.

BREAKING FREE

TEACHER'S GUIDE & WEBSITE

For Educators:

A *Teacher's Guide* is available online with resources and suggestions to help you incorporate **Breaking Free** into your curriculum. You'll find:

- **A Guide to Reading and Understanding the Book** with lists of questions to help students delve into and more fully explore the lives of Somaly Mam, Minh Dang, and Maria Suarez
- **Questions and Exercises for the Class** — Suggested assignments for students, either individually or in groups, that will foster interaction and discussion in the classroom
- **Terms to Define and Discuss**
- **Suggestions for Further Reading and Ways to Get Involved** — Resources to help students explore the issues in more depth

For Students:

The website is dedicated to **Breaking Free** so you can learn more about the survivors in the book and about trafficking in general. You'll find:

- In-depth biographies of Somaly Mam, Minh Dang, Maria Suarez, and the author
- Statistics that show the pervasiveness of human and sex trafficking in the world today
- Reader Reviews — a forum that will allow students to voice and share their opinions about the book and the issues with their peers
- Events — a list of author engagements and book signings

Visit *www.barronsbooks.com/breakingfree*